Marilyn Gibson

Hanging by a String

Hanging by a String

Marilyn Gibson

Writers Club Press
San Jose New York Lincoln Shanghai

Hanging by a String

All Rights Reserved © 2000 by Marilyn Gibson

No part of this book may be reproduced or transmitted in any form or by any means, graphic, electronic, or mechanical, including photocopying, recording, taping, or by any information storage or retrieval system, without the permission in writing from the publisher.

Writers Club Press
an imprint of iUniverse.com, Inc.

For information address:
iUniverse.com, Inc.
5220 S 16th, Ste. 200
Lincoln, NE 68512
www.iuniverse.com

The stories and events in this book are true. However, some names and details have been changed to protect the privacy of certain individuals.

ISBN: 0-595-14494-2

Printed in the United States of America

*To my father, Robert and my husband, Tim.
In loving memory of my mother, Ione.*

Contents

Introduction xi
The End and the Beginning 1
Awakenings 13
Beginnings 22
Discoveries 38
Journeys of Faith 48
Traveling to My Death 62
Alone 73
Pneumonia 80
Discoid 86
A Man Who Heals 96
Meningitis 122
An Exalted Master 129
First Kidney Involvement 133
Second Nephritis 141
Hemodialysis 148
Peritoneal Dialysis 161
Spiritual Healing 173

Remission	179
Dialysis Revisited	187
The Transplant	198
Home	208
Modern Medical Science and Healing	213
An End to Suffering	218

Acknowledgements

There are so many people whose encouragement empowered me to write this book:

Johanna Tacadena, my talented and wonderful friend, for encouraging me to bring the book together and then for her enthusiastic support in all phases of my writing.

Allan and Ellie Schiller, fellow violinists, for their support.

Seth Reichlin and Susie Melnick for their encouragement.

Linda Stux and Deb Simon for their enthusiastic endorsements which meant so much to me.

Janet Blazejowski, for her generous help in compiling the illustrations.

Teresa Austin and Larry Guy, for their editorial suggestions in the book's early stages.

Allan Brick, my extraordinary editor, who has been a mentor contributing his fine literary judgement, enthusiasm and skill.

Finally, I would like to express gratitude to my family. To my loving Aunt Louise, who helps me feel the spirit of my mother every day, and to my cousins Teresa and Debbie. To my brothers, Bob and Jeff. To my father, with gratitude I cannot name. You have given me life not once but twice. And, finally, to my husband, Tim, for staying with me throughout.

Introduction

I believe that we choose what we need throughout life to address lack in our souls. This includes disease. In fact, disease can be a most effective learning device. Through pain, we are forced to analyze our actions in an effort to find the source of our suffering. Only then can we move away from our disease patterns. In my case, disease appeared as a signpost which pointed to a road of discovery. This journey moved in several directions. It was to take me far from conventional knowledge.

My diagnosis of lupus erythematosus inaugurated a spiritual journey. The imperative to rid myself of the disease added urgency to my quest. Through the disease process, I experienced accelerating stages of awareness. Each manifestation of lupus brought me to a new understanding. At every stage, my road map altered. A new route emerged or a previous passage was defined with more accuracy. In the process of my journey, I discovered several spiritual keys to health. With the aid of these important tools, I was able to unlock the true nature of my soul that had been temporarily obscured through the disease process. Along the way, I glimpsed many beautiful visions and a near-death experience. My life as a violinist was guided by these encounters. Finally, with the aid of a successful transplant, I was able to clear away the need for disease. I present my journey in the hope that you, too, can find the answers you seek.

I.

The End and the Beginning

My head was splitting. A metallic taste had killed my appetite, yet my body had swollen to almost twice its size. Fluid crowding my lungs made each breath a struggle. Christmas was almost here. Just after dawn, an intern playing Santa scampered into my hospital room. "Merry Christmas! Ho Ho Ho!" he shouted. His laugh was earsplitting to my poisoned senses.

Santa reached into his red flannel bag and pulled out a green Sportsac. It was a nice gesture, though I was far beyond caring. The merry sounds bounced through my head like pots and pans in an amphitheater. I wanted to cry out but said nothing.

It was my third and final day of pulse therapy. One thousand milligrams of solumedrol, a derivative of cortisone, had been 'pulsed', or dripped through my IV in two daily doses. Cortisone supercedes the adrenal glands, which create 'fight or flight' reactions within the body. Receiving pulse therapy felt like an LSD trip combined with an overdose of amphetamines. Fireworks of hallucination exploded in my mind yet I was unable to move. I felt like a beached whale.

It was my fourth day without sleep, my third week of hospitalization. I was grateful that I had survived another night, though making it through each day was a torturing test of endurance. Sleepless night after night I barely held on to sanity as renal poisoning filled my body. The nights were the hardest as my mind circled helplessly, unable to find relief from the merciless pain.

Systemic Lupus Erythematosus had attacked my kidneys. Pulse therapy, this diabolical megadose of cortisone, had been prescribed as a last resort. I had responded to cortisone in the past. If some was effective, the doctors reasoned, more would be better. My body should have been traumatized into compliance, but it wasn't happening. This Christmas I held tightly to the roller coaster bar in front of me, terrified that with a slip I would fly off and hurtle to the ground. As I fought on, the world distorted with bizarre images leading me to the darkest corners of my mind. Through a haze of pain I repeated the twenty-third Psalm and the Lord's Prayer hundreds of times. I was dimly aware that I must dig my way out of this dilemma although it was far from the first time in my life that I had experienced a life-threatening crisis.

For seventeen years, I had often kept lupus at bay. The summer after my nineteenth birthday I had been diagnosed with lupus. I was overworked and striving for a degree in violin. It was my destiny to become a violinist. I knew this because of a revelation I had received several years before.

I was sixteen. One summer afternoon, as I sat reading, I was listening to a Mozart concerto. My southern Baptist upbringing encouraged followers of Christ to be devoted and emotional. The book was *Quo Vadis*, a stirring account of the earliest Christians. It resonated deep within me, strengthening my faith.

The sun began to wane, casting an amber glow on the knotty pine wall in front of me. A fresh scent emanated from the empty lot next door. As I settled deep into the plush couch, I finished *Quo Vadis* and cried for those crucified for their faith.

My father had won a Stromberg-Carlsen stereo in a nationwide contest. Dad loved great music, and he acquired fine recordings by such celebrated performers such as Jascha Heifetz. This afternoon I had selected the Mozart A Major Concerto (The "Turkish") performed by Isaac

Stern. My soul soared with Mozart's music and Stern's exquisite sound. *In a heartbeat, the room became an ocean of blue sky. Silver clouds tumbled across, obscuring the wall in front of me. It dazzled like no earthly sky, and it enveloped me. I floated somewhere inside, completely unaware of my own presence. Here the only reality was bliss, purity of sound and perfect harmony. Mozart, through Isaac Stern's violin, had taken me there. I do not know how long it lasted, minutes or hours. At the end I sat in the dark, my body humming—saturated with stillness far beyond words. Music had unlocked a heavenly gate that had transported me beyond the dimensions of reality.*

This sublime journey was surely a message sent by heavenly forces. If music had brought me to this realm, it was possible that others could have the same experience. My mission was clear. I would reveal my vision to others and the price of entrance would be the sweet tone of the violin! I gravitated toward this perfect sky as a parched man is to an oasis. I would follow wherever it led me.

Now, seventeen years after my diagnosis, lupus was visiting me vigorously. I was battling for my life. My kidneys were shutting down, refusing to eliminate the toxins that accumulated with deathly certainty.

The renal diet was set in front of me three times a day. I looked at the unappetizing fare and forced a few bites. Because the toxins created a metallic aftertaste, nothing was as I remembered it. Renal poisoning grabbed me like the worst hangover, one that never let go. The pain was merciless. Through a mental fog, I struggled to grasp the magnitude of my dilemma.

My room was a tiny hovel with no ventilation. Two beds barely fit. More than two visitors made it impossibly crowded. My bed faced a mottled yellow-brown wall, a fitting image for the agony of my incarceration. I would scrutinize its fine points through many sleepless nights.

That night, as usual, my husband Tim, a Juilliard-trained flutist, had trekked across town after his evening performance to spend hours at my bedside. His face was rosy and cold to the touch and I kissed his sensuous mouth, feeling his thick mustache against my lips. He drew back, looking quite himself. His slate blue eyes, framed by long, languid lashes and a patrician nose, emphasized a masculinity that was tempered and refined. Here was that air of quiet dignity that often intimidated his colleagues. As he took off his coat, I managed a smile. He frowned, scrutinizing me.

"Could you refresh my washcloth, please?" I whispered. Tim went to the small sink and soaked my washcloth in cold water. He placed it on my forehead. I attempted a smile but the knifelike sensation just behind my eyes commanded my attention. I froze to avoid further pain.

He presented me with a small velvet box. I roused myself to open it. "Oh, Tim!" I gasped. The gift, a pair of peridot earrings embedded with a tiny diamond, was exquisite. I could not hold back the tears. "You'll wear them soon," he assured me. I nodded without conviction. He handed me a small video game. "Here's something to pass the time." I attempted to play but my mind refused to concentrate. It was a sad little Christmas. As Tim sat quietly at my bedside I took his hand and wished he could take the suffering away. I relished the comfort of his presence, trying desperately to believe that this ordeal would soon be over, but I knew with a sad resignation that it was not to be so.

After visiting hours were over and I was left alone, throughout each sleepless night I was granted no respite from the constant bustle, glaring light and lack of privacy in the hospital. Somehow, it seemed that few of the medical professionals observing me empathized with my condition. Near death, with no sleep, no food, and my body ballooned up to twice its size, I did not have the strength to call out my agony.

It was almost midnight. Dr. Charles Christian slipped into my room. His silver hair and chiseled features had caused many patients heartthrobs. He was a statuesque man, the sort who graces magazine covers. I had always pictured him in a pilot's uniform. As head of Internal Medicine, he was a busy doctor. A renowned authority on lupus, he treated many patients, taught, and chaired several hospital committees.

The hours he kept were brutal. He often popped in my room as late as midnight and before seven a.m. the next day he could be seen leading eager interns through his morning rounds.

"You have a very high fever and hemolytic anemia," he informed me. "Your white blood cell count is abnormally high. I would like to give you a transfusion to help us out of this lethal anemia, but there is a probability that the lupus will attack the red blood cells in the transfused blood." I listened through a haze of pain.

"What are you going to do, Doctor?"

"We're not sure, Marilyn. We will remove the fluid crowding your lungs through dialysis. I'm afraid it's necessary."

"You're telling me," I wheezed.

"Then we will locate some blood without too many vulnerable antibodies. That will be difficult."

"Okay," I said. Was there a choice? "Thank you, Doctor." I was torn. The diseases, the therapies, were so abhorrent. Yet, I was grateful for the treatments. I felt like a masochistic saying, "Please, Sir. May I have another?"

Through a daze, I reflected upon our complex relationship. I had often been an exasperating patient, waiting until the disease had brought its usual symptoms of a low-grade fever and general malaise before consulting him. Doctor Christian had saved my life on more than one occasion. I had every reason to believe that I was safe through this harrowing experience. If I must be here, I was glad to be among the finest doctors in the world. Yet, after each visit with Dr. Christian I felt ineffectual. His smooth professional demeanor was a stark contrast to my state as a helpless patient. I was the child and Dr. Christian was the father. In a few short weeks, I had zoomed from accomplished professional to helpless patient at the bottom of the hospital hierarchy. As my health careened out of control and my body ballooned out of proportion, I felt smaller and smaller. Was I Marilyn Gibson, violinist, or was I a set of symptoms defined as lupus nephritis with hemolytic anemia and viral involvement? While this technical classification was entirely necessary, my status as a deeply wounded human being was ignored.

Now, with Dr. Christian's departure, I was alone. The crisis kept increasing. Hospitalized already for two weeks, and getting worse! *Suddenly a white trap door appeared on the wall in front of me. This clapboard storm cellar slanted at an angle from the ground. The shadowy figure trapped inside almost broke it down with his powerful lunges. I shoved him down with every ounce of my dwindling strength. Somehow, I knew that to catch his eye was to invite disaster, but as I bolted the door, I stole a glimpse of his ugly face.*

He fell into the cellar. I had won the first round. Diabolically, the demon had chosen my friend Max's form. He was attempting to gain my trust but I wasn't fooled. This force of blackest evil was intent on killing me. It would take my soul and my body, too, if I did not fight with every ounce of strength I had.

We grappled the entire night. The wraith was tireless. He would not desist until he could lay claim to me. My panic exacerbated by the drugs, I felt completely alone. Though pain had affected my reasoning ability, it seemed obvious that this monstrous visitor was an amalgam of my many mistakes, very much here alive and kicking. Negative actions had congregated like barnacles to form this hideous creature. If the apparition prevailed I would either die or descend into psychosis, a known side effect of steroid doses that are intolerably high. Hellish worlds of distortion loomed as I braced myself for a lengthy combat with my dark side.

The battle raged on. I was flirting with death, but this was no pleasant near-death encounter at the end of a golden tunnel. As I later learned, this shadowy form was the malevolent disease assaulting my body; my kidneys were being irreparably damaged. Repeatedly I recited "The Lord is My Shepherd..." invoking the power of Christ for help in my battle. These simple words held a promise of assistance from above. As my mind bounced off the claustrophobic walls, the psalm aided my desperate fight for control.

Breathing was becoming impossible. To distract myself I put a cassette tape in my Walkman. Tim had given me a Christmas album of the jazz a cappella group *Take Six*. At any other time, I might admire their artistry, but not tonight. Their style was kinetic, not soothing. Still I clung to the majestic world of music. Maybe here I would find the calm I sought. Anything to transport me somewhere else. However, it was no use. Not even music could take away the pain.

My mind circled helplessly in a holding pattern as I counted the minutes until light dawned. Four a.m. approached and five a.m. seemed miles away. The hospital team changed to the day shift at six a.m. I breathed a sigh of relief when the morning nurse came to weigh me. The hours of suffering were over, but five nights of sleeplessness had accumulated.

"Good morning!" A cheery morning nurse snapped on the overhead light. I thrust a wet washcloth over my eyes.

"It's time to weigh you," she ordered. "Sit up. Stand on this scale."

I could not move. Because of the fluid retention near my lungs, turning to my side was excruciating. Swollen beyond recognition, my legs would not budge.

"Oh dear," she clucked, scuttling the scale to my roommate. "I'll be back soon."

Soon two hulking orderlies appeared dragging a giant scale. This contraption consisted of metal bars attached to a cradle-like leather sack. It reminded me of the stork's diaper that brings new arrivals into the world. As the men hoisted me on to the sack swaying in midair, I screamed out in pain. I felt ashamed of my helplessness and I was so naked under my flimsy hospital gown.

After this humiliating experience, the 'vampire nurse' arrived. She checked my arm bracelet and extracted ten tubes of blood. This amount was removed twice a day. I marveled that the fount never seemed to run dry.

"Is this absolutely necessary?" I protested.

"Doctor's orders," she barked. "Besides, the amount is inconsequential. It's quickly replaced."

After the early intrusions were temporarily at an end, and with the encircling curtains removed, I became conscious of my roommate. Mrs. Smith was an eighty-six-year-old black woman with firm chocolate skin that belied her age. She described her apartment in the Bronx with pride, believing that she would soon return home. When a leg injury had immobilized her, she was admitted to this room until the social system could decide where to send her. Each night at hourly intervals she would yell, "My leg! My leg!" until the nurses came. It was like the boy who cried "Wolf!" My roommate had worn the nurses' patience thin, though she was oblivious to that fact. She was frequently ignored but this caused no cessation of complaints.

"Now Marilyn, honey," she would say. "Don't worry a bit. Soon you'll be home and just fine." I had wanted to believe her. I had wanted to awaken from this horrible nightmare and find that everything was as before, but I was now slipping past the decisive point. Even if I survived, life would never be the same. Lupus nephritis had almost killed me. My failing kidneys were leaking protein and the diuretic intended to lessen fluid retention was not working.

The hospital procedure throughout the day was simple. After early monitoring routines, the nurses changed the bed before breakfast. My body had become so bloated that I could not muster the energy to bathe myself. The caring nurses at Special Surgery soothed my bedsores with liniment and powder.

A nurse's aide from Puerto Rico named Maria had a kind word or a special treat for me each day. She treated me like her own child. This morning she brought an exquisite flower arrangement.

"Did you make that?" I asked.

"Yes. For you." I was touched.

"Now, you will be fine, Marilyn," she soothed. "My niece was on dialysis for awhile. Then she got a transplant, and you should see her! She is beaooootiful! So it will work out," she exclaimed in a thick accent, patting my hand.

This success story sparked a faint glimmer of hope, premature though it was. I had not accepted the possibility of dialysis and a transplant was inconceivable. When the haze of pain cleared long enough for me to think, I sobbed at the thought of my future life. Maria's morning gift had helped to lighten my burden. I was grateful for her loving concern.

My compassionate nurses often gave me a soothing bath, a wet washcloth for my throbbing head, or an ice cream treat in the middle of the night. Our connection of love and faith created a healing balm for me. This was the human touch that was missing from my relationship with the doctors. I sensed that the doctors knew this. They depended upon these efficient nurses for the routine tasks of ministering to sick bodies and carrying out their orders. This balance made the brutality of the IV's, the megasteroids, blood taking and absence of sleep a little easier to bear.

Doctor Christian realized that I would not last much longer. One of the Special Surgery nurses now told me that he had ordered two transfusions to stave off the anemia. The doctor worried that I would make antibodies to this new blood, and hovered over me for hours in my tiny room. I was impressed. Now, as the morning advanced, instead of spending the holidays with his family, he was here checking me for a reaction to the transfusion. It was a strange scene. I reclined helplessly in bed. Tim had come to visit again and now sat by my side as Dr. Christian stood in front of the yellow-brown wall watching me. Tim nodded as the doctor explained that the team physician for the football team playing on television was an acquaintance. In spite of the small talk, I sensed that Tim and the doctor were alarmed. My breathing was a terrifying struggle and the pulse therapy had not worked. I felt powerless against the attacking force. It was winning.

After the doctor left, I took my husband's hand. Poor Tim! Rushing back to the hospital each night after performing Christmas music, he found his wife barely able to move or breathe. The chasm created by my dilemma was deep. Though he could not know my agony, Tim sat by me hour after hour, comforting me through the long days so that I could muster the strength to survive the painful nights.

Suddenly an orderly appeared and wheeled my bed to the hall near the nurse's station.

"What's going on?" Tim asked.

"Marilyn has been ordered to go for a sonogram," he announced.

"I should go, too," Tim frowned.

"You don't have to," I said uncertainly, not quite ready to release him

"I have a lot to do at home. I'll be back tomorrow."

"All right," I sighed, steeling myself to endure the hours ahead. Here in the bustling heart of the ward, the light and noise were unbearable.

"I'm nauseous," I whispered.

"You'll have to speak up, dear," a nurse replied. She gave me a kidney-shaped (what irony!) plastic dish. My heightened awareness had amplified every noise, each blinding ray of light. I wanted to cry out my distress. Yet the busy doctors and nurses an arm's length away seemed oblivious to my dilemma.

Waiting is the patient's job. Waiting, powerless helplessness. I lifted the wet washcloth from my eyes to assess the scene. Busily dispensing treatments, studying charts, socializing, they were unaware of me. I was invisible. On public display and without sleep or nourishment, I was at the mercy of a nameless orderly who was taking his time. By now, I was nearly delirious with high fever. With the bustle around me tuned to a high pitch, it was impossible for the staff to hear my silent cry for help.

Finally, I went for an abdominal sonogram. The procedure took place in a blissfully dim, quiet room. Cold jelly was spread over my abdomen and a wand rubbed over my stomach as I viewed my organs on a television screen. It was a pleasant sensation, which provided an interlude from the interminable hours in bed. Afterwards, I was deposited in the hall with a chart on my stomach. Fortunately, this hallway was deserted. I had relaxed enough to doze off for the first time in days.

Then I awakened to find my friends Mary Rowell and Sarah Carter grinning down at me. I rubbed my eyes. Was I hallucinating? "What are you doing here? How did you find me so far away from my room?" I croaked.

"The nurses told us you had gone for a test. We found you on the map, so here we are." I marveled at Mary Rowell. Standing six feet tall, her hair was an unruly mass of Shirley Temple curls. She was an oversized pixie. A violinist who trained at Juilliard, she also played electric bass in her own rock band. We had met through an ensemble called *Festival Strings*. Mary had founded the group and had written most of the arrangements of classical, popular music and jazz. Locating remote schools for *Festival Strings* performances had been easy for her. The catacombs of the New York Hospital posed no challenge.

When Mary decided to leave the group, she passed the violin position to me. One spring several years before, I had been offered a cruise in the Caribbean and asked Sarah Carter, the group's cellist, to come along. After many intimate talks, Sarah became a lifelong friend. Mary smiled and presented me with a red velveteen elephant. "This will keep you company."

I was touched. "Thanks, Mary!" I hugged my new friend. The name Rachel popped into my mind. It was a Biblical name. Somehow, my little red elephant seemed like a Rachel.

"Rachel," I said softly. "I'll call her Rachel." I loved stuffed animals. What a thoughtful gift! Especially now, when I needed something, anything, to hug through the endless nights. I smiled through a haze of pain, hospital confinement, and fear for my future. My colleagues possessed no frame of reference for these feelings. The familiar gap between my friends and myself yawned before me. None of them had experienced anything like this.

After seventeen years of battling to cure myself, it seemed that the disease had won. My odyssey had taken me across this country and to Europe. In seeking to define the nature of the disease, I had discovered the teachings of Buddhism, Yoga, Edgar Cayce and mystic Christianity. Throughout my struggle, I sought to maintain the normal health I considered my birthright. The gap between my healthy friends and me could be narrowed if I were to discover the keys that would unlock the hidden causes of my situation. I would search my past. Surely, there I would find the solution that would bring me to safety.

II.

Awakenings

"Mom—"

"What, Marl?"

"What's that red stuff on your face?"

"They call it a butterfly rash, honey. It is from lupus, which means 'wolf'. They say I have it."

The splotches on her nose and cheeks looked like a butterfly, though not a very pretty one. "Why did you get it, Mommy?"

She sighed. "I don't know, sweetheart. I'll have to wait for it to go away and take cortisone, like the doctor says."

Mother was 35 when she discovered she had lupus. During this summer of 1962, she had had lupus for three years. Her symptoms were the butterfly rash, a low fever and anemia. At times she was compelled to rest, to stay in bed all day, until the fever abated. I was ten, only dimly aware that her life more difficult because of these bouts. I would find out much later that women in their childbearing years are at the highest risk for lupus, and that it turned the body against itself. This autoimmune disease could affect virtually every organ in the body, but particularly the kidneys. Lupus could also damage the lungs and heart and cause neuralgic symptoms.

Yet, in spite of her struggles with lupus, my mother seemed larger than life. As her only daughter, I enjoyed a close relationship with her, but she brought joy to everyone who knew her. Her talent and warmth were legendary.

Ione George was a prodigy in the small town of Weems, Virginia. She could pick up any instrument and play a tune. In 1933, when she was ten years old, she learned the mandolin and entered an amateur contest with her six-year-old sister Louise. Louise sang *Go Long, Mule* to Ione's accompaniment. To her surprise, they won. Ione was a sickly child. She often stayed home from school and it was at these times that she discovered music, entertaining herself for hours on the piano and the mandolin. When it became clear that her abilities were extraordinary Nellie Bly George, her mother, took her to the best piano teacher she could find. Russell MacMeans lived on the road between Kilmarnock and Irvington. Nellie heard that he had played in a big city years ago. Ione hoped that one day, she, too, would perform in exotic places far from Weems. Today she would play Chopin, then she would sing. Mr. MacMeans taught both. She often said that the birds sang especially well during the drive to her lesson, for inspiration. At other times there were storms near the water. The fierce winds, the blinding rain, the lightning that seemed to strike so close, motivated her to capture this turbulence in her playing.

Iredel, her father, saved his money and bought a 48-bass accordion that Ione played for recitals and musical programs. She was always glad to share the music that flowed so effortlessly from her—old favorites like the *Gypsy Love Song* and Lehar's *My Hero*.

Carter's Creek flowed in front of her home. This tributary fed the Rappahanock, which emptied into the Chesapeake Bay a few miles down river. When Ione was seventeen, she and Louise, who was thirteen, attended a dance at the Community Hall. Although these events occurred every week, this was Louise's first dance. That afternoon they had set their hair in pin curls. After supper was over, Nannie said, "Now, you go and rest, Ione. You've done too much already. Get yourself ready for the dance. Louise, you help with the dishes."

"Yes, Mama," Louise sighed as Ione went upstairs to her bedroom. She fell into bed, letting the refreshing summer breeze cool her. She had dozed off when she felt Louise's hand on her shoulder.

"Don't you want to go to the dance, Ione?"

"Oh. I guess I fell asleep."

"You did practice all day. Remember?"

Ione sat up, checking her alarm clock. "We'd better hurry! What am I going to wear?" She went to the mahogany closet and picked her favorite off-the-shoulder blouse, a flared black-and-red-print skirt and red sandals. Louise had already changed into a plaid skirt with a light sweater.

"Don't stay out late, Ione," Nannie warned. "You have a lesson tomorrow."

"Yes, Mama." The sisters set off down the dirt road, becoming silent as they approached the center of Weems. The Rappahannock glistened in the distance as the full moon cast silver shadows that danced over the waves.

"Do you think we'll meet anyone?" Louise asked, her red hair bouncing with new curls. Ione grasped her chin.

"Too much lipstick," she frowned. "I shouldn't have let you tag along."

"I'm old enough," Louise pouted. "Mama says so."

"Only because I talked her into it. If I weren't going, you wouldn't either."

"Oh, phooey," Louise scoffed, grinding a saddle oxford into the sand.

Ione laughed. "Don't worry, Louise. We will have a wonderful time. You'll see." Most of the time she went barefoot in the summer. These sandals were cutting her feet. She was glad they were almost there.

Light streamed out of The Community Hall, an oblong white building near the Presbyterian Church. Big band music drifted into the lane. Ione's foot started to tap in spite of pinched toes. She squeezed her sister's hand. "Now don't go off, Louise. We have to be home in two hours."

"Oh, all right," Louise sighed. Ione paid fifty cents while Louise made straight for the punch table. Before Ione could manage to greet her girlfriends, a young man approached her. "Hi, Ione," he said. His brown eyes met hers. Robert Gibson was tall and slim with a prominent nose, thin lips and wavy brown hair. Almost twenty-one, he was considerably older than her usual dates. His dashing manner and dark good looks reminded her of Tyrone Power.

"I enjoyed hearing you at the talent show," he said. "You play beautifully."

"Why, thank you," she replied. "It's nice of you to say so. However, that was some time ago. You still remember it?"

"Of course. I have just bought a small accordion but I haven't learned the first tune yet. You wouldn't consider giving me lessons, would you?"

"Why, all right." Ione nodded, trying to sound confident.

"Would you like this dance?"

Ione glanced around the hall, checking for Thomas Lawson, her steady beau. There was no trace of him. She hesitated, then tossed her head defiantly.

"Yes, I believe I will," she smiled. They began to dance. Robert was light on his feet. As they floated across the floor, she stole a glance at her companion. Her memory of Thomas Lawson was fading rapidly.

Ione knew of Robert and his family in Kilmarnock, the next town over from White Stone. His father Herbert had been the pastor of the Kilmarnock Baptist Church. Robert had graduated from Kilmarnock High School. He had two equally handsome brothers. Ione was surprised that Robert was interested in her. She was four years younger. However, his attentiveness and gentlemanly behavior quickly erased any doubts she had.

Robert often came to call at the house on the point overlooking Carter's Creek. Nellie and Iredel approved of the handsome young man as a good match for their daughter. Ione found herself falling in love.

They always had a good time. Ione was fun to be with and Robert had a great sense of humor.

During the second summer of their courtship, Ione performed Victor Herbert's *Indian Love Call* for a large, enthusiastic crowd. Though she was not the prettiest girl Robert had dated, she was the only one who could transport him to another world with her singing and playing. Not having had the benefit of music training himself, he had always felt a lack of talent. He marveled at the ease Ione displayed in delivering the lush romantic scores and joined in the enthusiastic applause at the end.

In 1941, Ione graduated from the White Stone High School. Soon afterwards, he asked her to marry him. After the war began, Robert enlisted in the Marines. Although they were engaged, he knew the uncertainty of war and did not feel that they should marry until afterwards. Ione moved to Baltimore to help in the war effort and worked as a secretary in a shipyard.

On his last leave before shipping out to the Pacific, he traveled from the West Coast on a fifteen-day furlough—just enough time to get from California to Baltimore and back. Robert was happy to see Ione, but he still resisted the idea of wartime marriages. Better to leave things the way they were. Ione did not agree. She knew that he might never come back, but she had made a life-long commitment. Robert was the only man she would ever want.

"It's now or never," she told him. "We've been engaged for two years. If you put this off again, we're through."

Robert felt coerced into a decision that would require some hard thinking, but he could not ignore this ultimatum. His mother Julia, who had been a widow since Robert was thirteen, needed him. He knew that she would not be pleased, but he went ahead. The couple was married on Easter Day, 1944, in Baltimore, and the next day they drove down to his mother's home in Kilmarnock. Julia and Robert conversed about the war and politics, their favorite subject. Hours passed as Ione waited in the small bedroom. Finally, Julia's dutiful son went to his bride.

After a three-day honeymoon, Ione saw Robert off for the long trip back to California. Almost two years would pass before he returned from the war. Robert's Marine division raised the flag at Iwo Jima; and, finally, in January of 1946 he came home.

Ione loved children and always wanted her own. Louise had met a handsome machinist named Franklin before the war. When his tour of duty with the Navy ended, they were married. Their first child, Debbie, was born and Ione visited frequently.

Robert and Ione began a new life, settling down in a small apartment in Richmond. He worked at a few odd jobs before taking a position as an insurance investigator for the Life Insurance Company of Virginia. Though it was not combat duty, investigating claims could be unpleasant. The neighborhoods were unsavory, the clients often surly. Robert was promoted and his new investigation job took him to other states. Ione often accompanied him on his trips. Soon, able to afford the nice clothes she could not afford as a poor country girl, she had accumulated a stylish wardrobe.

They were a gregarious couple and made friends everywhere they went. At each stop Ione doted on the small children she encountered, clutching them close. Robert took up photography and documented their journeys.

Though she loved to travel, her heart remained with the creeks and rivers of Tidewater. Although she would live in many states in later years, she always loved the water that was so much a part of the Chesapeake country. When she was there, it seemed to pour directly into her heart and replenish her soul. To return home was to nourish that special place of joy where music lived.

She visited frequently, especially in the summer when Robert was working in the big cities of his territory. On hot summer evenings, from her corner bedroom in the house on Carter's Creek, the wind in the trees and the soothing rhythm of the cicadas lulled her to sleep. Moreover, there was nothing like a good fishing trip or crabbing expedition with Louise to remind her of the things she loved down home.

One evening, Nellie Bly (Nannie to her relatives) sat on her front porch shelling butter beans as Louise rocked Debbie, her red hair catching the last rays of the afternoon sun.

Suddenly, Ione raced up the steps and burst through the screen door. "Louise!"

"What? What is it, for heaven's sake?"

"There's an opening at the Tides Inn for an organist and singer! An audition! I'm going to try out."

"But, you can't, Ione. You've never played the organ before."

"I can learn. How difficult can it be?"

"That's true. You can play anything." Louise sighed.

Ione sank into a nearby rocker. "It's boiling!" she exclaimed.

"I know, but the sun's going down. It'll ease soon."

The exclusive Tides Inn was an international resort across Carter's Creek. In the early evening, before the mosquitoes came, Ione often lounged in the hammock between the mammoth trees on the point. From the time she was a girl, she had seen the affluent clientele across the creek playing golf and sunning at the pool. She would try out. And she would win. The next morning she put on a suit and borrowed Louise's car to drive to the Inn.

"I'm Ione Gibson. I'd like to try out for your position as organist and singer."

The manager raised his eyebrow in a quick assessment. After a moment, he nodded. "Go through that door," he said, pointing.

"This takes some nerve," she thought, walking into the empty dining room. "But what a beautiful Hammond," she noted, running her fingers over the keys. "If they only knew I've never played one before," she laughed to herself as she began to explore the instrument. "Pedals and stops for different effects. I see." After thirty minutes, she emerged. "I'd like to play for you now," she said.

"Certainly." The manager followed her through the swinging doors and sat down at a skirted table. Ione played, the tunes flowing smoothly into one another. Twenty minutes passed before the manager spoke.

"Thank you," he said. Then silence. Ione held her breath.

"Mrs. Gibson, that is beautiful organ playing. You've got the job."

"Oh, thank you, thank you!"

"You'll start with lunch and dinner tomorrow."

"Wonderful. I'll see you then!"

As Ione came down the lane, dirt flying, Louise and Nannie rose from their rockers. Louise hugged her sister. "Of course you got the job. We could hear you from across the creek."

Attractive and talented, Ione was a sensation at the Tides Inn. When Robert returned from his trip Ione could hardly wait to greet him with the good news.

"Robert," she began slowly, "We never got a real honeymoon." She paused, searching his face for a reaction. Seeing none, she continued. "We stayed at your mother's."

"I know, Ione. She needed me."

"Of course…But now that you have some time off, let's stay at the Tides Inn! I have an employee's discount, and you can play golf. How about it?"

They stayed at the Inn for two weeks. Ione was the local girl who had become something of a celebrity. Afterwards Robert returned to Richmond. Ione stayed with Nannie and continued to play at the Inn.

One evening Ione was lounging at the pool between sets when a dark, bespectacled man in an expensive suit approached them. He introduced himself as Richard Fried, adding that he was an entertainment agent in New York. He went on. "You're quite a singer, Ione."

"Why, thank you." Ione smiled.

"I am also impressed with your organ playing. I think you could make it in New York. We could set you up with an orchestra. I handle singers. Though I cannot make a solid commitment, I do have many venues. You would have a real chance at the big time."

"Your offer is tempting, Mr. Fried. I must admit that I'm flattered." Silently, she weighed the alternatives. "But I'm afraid I can't accept."

"Why not?"

"I'm a happily married woman. My husband comes first."

"Think about it. You're very talented."

"Thank you, but my first allegiance is to Robert."

"Well, here's my card. Call me if you change your mind."

Ione had made a life-changing decision, and soon her sacrifice would be rewarded. Her dream of motherhood was about to come true.

III.

Beginnings

I arrived in October of 1951. Robert's job as insurance investigator still required travel, but it was difficult with an infant. I had the colic and kept Mother up most nights. Having quit her Tides Inn job when she became pregnant, she felt alone in the small apartment when Robert was gone most of the time. Therefore, Mother took me down home for my first Christmas. Nannie doted on her second grandchild while Ione shared the joys of motherhood with Louise. Ione was glad her pregnancy had come so soon after Mr. Fried's offer. It gave her less time to mourn the fact that she had given up her Tides Inn position and a chance at fame. Nannie was happy to have her girls reunited. In the evenings, they gathered at the baby grand to sing hymns and carols.

Dad's next position was as an Agent in Toledo, Ohio of the Life of Virginia, and later to Michigan. After the arrival of my brother Bob in 1953, Mother devoted herself to raising Bob and me. Every Sunday, dressed in finery that Mother had created, we attended the Baptist church. Robert was always there with the camera. A year later, a position as Assistant Manager opened in Baltimore, and we moved again. We bought a row house. Thrilled to be a homeowner for the first time, Mother decorated it lovingly, painting whole rooms in a day. We bought furniture and an upright piano. My brother Jeffrey was born in 1955, yet even with three toddlers Mother found time to play.

I loved musicals. "*The Music Man*" was my favorite. I recited the entire record, making up my own choreography. When I was six Mother began to teach me piano. She bought me the John Thompson method and helped me with my note reading. I spent hours improvising, trying to imitate her flourishes and her arpeggios. It seemed so easy when Mother did it, but I could only play one note at a time. This process was entirely too slow for me. When I was six, during a session with my Mother, I had a tantrum. "I don't want piano lessons!" I screamed, jutting out my lower lip and stomping my foot. Mother threw up her hands. "I've had enough, Marilyn. I cannot teach you any more. I'll have to get you someone else."

My new teacher, Mr. McFawber, was ancient. He had snow-white hair and towered over Mother like the abominable snowman. He eclipsed me on the piano bench. There were red lines on his cheeks and brown dots on his huge hands. He wore the same black suit each week, appearing as if he had come from a funeral. Mr. McFawber's book of choice was also John Thompson's Piano Instruction, a big red-and-white book with songs such as '*Lightly Row*'. Although he said very little, he had one unusual habit. At each lesson, he drew a hand next to the staff that pointed to passages I needed to practice. Except for my Grandmother Gibson, I had never met anyone so old. Though he was patient and not unkind, after a few lessons, my vivid imagination created a new scenario. I pictured him dropping dead during my lesson. Indeed, one day, during my performance of a passage next to his drawing of a hand, I imagined he was stricken with a heart attack. Slouching over the keys of my piano, his bloodshot eyes stayed wide open as his face hit the keys and stayed there—Middle C etched permanently into his forehead. Fortunately, my lack of practice did not kill him, although our acquaintance was short-lived.

Dad was promoted to Agency Manager and we moved to Terre Haute, Indiana. One day a short, bald man named Jerome Fougerousse came into my classroom. His face was shaped like his body—small at both ends and round in the middle. He wore a light tan suit and carried an assortment of musical instruments. My third grade teacher, Mrs. Beaver, devoted the entire fourth period to him. I listened to his descriptions without interest until, suddenly, he held high a tiny violin. It had a curved shape and a glossy shine. There were two holes in the middle shaped like the letter 's'. The chestnut color reminded me of my mother's best coffee table that she polished regularly with Pledge. This violin was a small size, Mr. Fougerousse said, for little people like me. Originally I had wanted to play the clarinet, but when he looked at my bottom teeth, he shook his head.

"No, they're too crooked," he said, peering at me through half-moon glasses as two lonely hairs sprouted from the top of his bald head. "You will not be able to play the clarinet."

Then Mr. Fougerousse played. His sound was exquisite. It was like my mother's singing voice—lilting and full. I wanted to know how I could make that sound, too. This instrument was so different from the piano. It was small and could easily be carried. Instead of learning the left-hand accompaniment, as with the piano, I only had to play one note at a time. With this violin I could play music, but at the same time do something entirely different from Mother. This was for me. That night I took the violin home and gingerly removed it from the case. I drew the bow behind the bridge. A grating, screeching noise emanated from my new instrument. Unfortunately, Mother heard it from the living room.

"What is that strange sound?" I shrank from her comment, realizing that I had no idea how to play the thing. Even so, I sensed the promise of my new friend. It would take me to places my mind and heart had fancied—the world of illusion to which I often escaped through reading or listening to music.

Once a week Mother drove me across town to my private violin lessons. In addition to teaching in the schools, Mr. Fougerousse taught privately and was concertmaster of the Terre Haute Symphony. It was almost an hour's trip. His home, a bungalow like much of the architecture in the older section of town, seemed just right for Mr. Fougerrousse's wife. Small and square like the house, she had rosy cheeks and was always smiling. The waiting room next to Mr. Fougerousse's studio contained an impressive selection of comic books. Then, in the teaching studio itself, there was a huge walk-in closet. Violins of every size hung from the walls. Unfortunately, achieving a good sound on the violin proved more difficult than I thought. The violin did not have the natural intonation of the piano. My progress was slow, but Mother made me practice. When I tried to cheat, she always caught me.

"Marilyn, you have fifteen minutes to go!"

"But, Mom!"

"No 'buts'! Get to it!"

The action of Mother's disease was sporadic. It was limited to low-grade fevers, anemia and the lupus rash over the cheeks and bridge of the nose. Her diagnosis was an adjustment for Robert, but as the years passed and nothing serious occurred, he took it in stride. He was devoted to her, though they often fought about things many couples dispute – money, and occasionally, religious preferences. As all three of us grew out of the toddler stages, Mother had more time for her music. She put together huge blue notebooks with hundreds of popular songs called 'fake books'. On many nights we went to the Elks Club, where we drank cokes, danced the twist, and listened to her perform. My rowdy brothers played tag under the tables and bothered the Elks, but Mother never seemed to mind. Occasionally she asked me to sing with her. I loved to take the microphone. It was easy to recall the words. Tunes like *Autumn Leaves* and *My Man* seemed a part of me—I had heard them since I was in the womb.

By the sixth grade, I had taught myself the organ. My earlier piano instruction proved helpful and soon I was playing many of the tunes Mother played. Bob learned the drums and we formed a little combo that performed for guests at my parents' parties.

In the summer, Mr. Fougerousse came to my house for the lessons. Though the heat was stifling, he always wore his tan suit and removed the jacket to reveal a rotund belly. Often Mother found me in our backyard just as he was arriving.

"Mr. Fougerousse is here! And look at your hands. They are filthy. He will not be pleased with those long fingernails! Marilyn, you know this is your lesson day. Why weren't you ready?" she shouted from the back door. I quickly ran in and washed my hands, finding Mr. Fougerousse waiting for me. After our lesson, Mother pointed to the organ.

"Marilyn, play *Jesu, Joy of Man's Desiring* for Mr. Fougerousse," she beamed. "You know, Marilyn is a fine organist. Show your teacher, Marilyn."

"Yes, Mother." I stole a glance at his shiny head as I played. It was glistening from the heat. I was certain that my teacher would prefer to be somewhere else. Nevertheless, he listened patiently.

"Very nice, Marilyn," he commented, his slight accent giving the compliment more authority.

However, after two years of private study, I still could not make the luscious violin sound Mother heard from Mr. Fougerousse's violin. She became impatient.

"Marilyn, when will you sound like Mr. Fougerousse?" she often said. I did not know how to reply. Even so, by the sixth grade I was selected to become the concertmaster of my elementary school orchestra. I was amazed that I had surpassed everyone. My family attended the concert and radiated pride during my solo with the orchestra.

During the summer of 1962, we enjoyed going to the Elks Country Club pool, where Mother worked on her tan. Our next-door-neighbor Betty Dunaway, one of Mother's many good friends, and her son Roger often joined us. That year she was cautioned to avoid the sun and, self-conscious about her rash, she wore a big straw hat for protection.

Every summer since I could remember, my family made the trip down home and stayed in Nannie's house on the point. In the morning, my brothers and I often went down to the wharf to check the pilings for crabs. Before long we were summoned by Nannie in her piercing voice from her kitchen window.

"Bobby! Jeffrey! Would you like scrapple or bacon with your eggs? Come get it before it gets cold!" We dropped what we were doing and ran up the hill as fast as we could. We didn't want to miss Nannie's eggs with the 'yelks', as she called them, dripping just right so that we could mop them up with white toast smothered in melted butter.

For lunch, we usually ate in Aunt Louise's kitchen, right next door to Nannie. She had fresh tomatoes from her garden which we sliced and seasoned with salt and pepper, as well as stewed tomatoes, greens with cider vinegar and crab cakes made with her own special recipe. If she had caught soft crabs that morning, she breaded them and fried them whole. Then she put them between two slices of Wonder Bread. In the evenings, we had Nannie's canned butter beans and bread pudding for dessert.

Occasionally we got together to 'pick crabs' in Nannie's back yard. After buying several dozen steamed crabs, Dad and Uncle Franklin covered the picnic table with newspapers and dumped the reddened crabs in the center. Mom and Aunt Louise set out pitchers of sweetened iced tea. Debbie, her little sister Teresa and I set the table, and the feast began. Using small knives, we dismantled the crab's outer shells and discarded their insides in search of the tender white meat. Uncle Franklin usually helped me get the meat—my crab-picking skills were not yet developed—after which I sprinkled Old Bay seasoning on the meat and dipped it in cider vinegar. A real Tidewater treat!

On Sundays, after church, we visited Grandmother Gibson in Kilmarnock where we had fresh biscuits she had made from scratch for Sunday dinner. Afterwards Dad and Grandmother Gibson retired to the living room where they discussed politics while we played in the front yard.

At the end of our two-week vacation we packed up the car and said tearful good-byes to Debbie and Teresa. On the two-day drive back to Terre Haute, Mother needed real patience not to respond when the three of us misbehaved in the back of our station wagon. We knew we were in trouble when, with reddened face, she turned slowly to face us from the front seat.

"When all three mouths are flapping at the same time, you can't hear your own ears!" she yelled. Chastened, we were silent for a few minutes. Then the fighting started again.

After we returned to Terre Haute Mother met another organist, Russ McCoy. He lived in the middle of town in a somewhat run-down Cape Cod. Russ and Dolly, his diminutive wife, had a daughter, Susan, and a son, Tommy, who was my age. Mother studied the organ with Russ, who played for a large church in the middle of town called the Methodist Temple. At the age of thirteen, I joined the church. Mother had not been comfortable with the "fire and brimstone," as she termed it, call to commitment at the end of the Baptist services. She preferred the Methodists' more genteel approach. Mother and I joined the choir. Dad even attended, and after church, we had hamburgers at one of the first McDonald's, across the street. Afterwards the adults had their treat as we visited Dad's retired secretary, Alice, and her omnipresent six-pack of Budweiser.

I had spent most of my childhood, from second grade to ninth, in Terre Haute. I was fourteen when we moved to Plainfield, a suburb of Indianapolis, Indiana. The year in Plainfield was difficult for making friends. I continued with the violin, but daily practice was a struggle. I loved the violin, but it was such a difficult instrument to learn. I had picked up the organ in a matter of months and had fun playing it. However, it seemed that every step towards mastery of the violin took great effort. I was just learning vibrato, a long and slow process that can take as long as a year, when I decided that I wanted to quit. I got the chance when Mother, busy with the move, decorated the new house. I also used this opportunity to stop practicing. I'm free! I thought gleefully, and as months passed, nothing was mentioned about a teacher. At first, I relished my freedom, painting my bedroom furniture and reading. However, after a few months I again longed for music in my life. One day I took the violin from its case and began the Seitz concerto, my last piece. I could not play it! My hiatus had resulted in a complete loss of skill. I had not realized that there was an intimate relationship between practicing and results. What a difficult thing this violin was! I decided I was not quite ready to enslave myself again.

After only one school year in Plainfield, Dad got a promotion to Life of Virginia's home office in Richmond. At the age of fifteen, I returned to the city of my birth. My hiatus from the violin had given me a new realization. I could not live without playing music. I needed the violin as I needed to breathe. Each of my rebellions against practicing—this latest one and my tantrum at the age of six, seemed ultimately to bring me closer to music. Because I had a choice, I ultimately realized the freedom within discipline that music brings.

The task of finding a teacher now fell upon me. One day I opened the yellow pages to Music Instruction and found my new teacher, Victorio Ceasare—who lived in an upscale suburb nearby. He was a swarthy Italian, short and chubby—all violinists seemed to have the same body type. I drove myself to lessons now. Mr. Ceasare was a patient teacher and an extraordinary violinist.

One day I brought him the Mendelssohn Concerto. I performed the difficult first movement and paused at the end for his comments. He's going to tell me I should quit, I thought. I knew the piece needed a lot of work. However, when I glanced at him I realized that he was staring at me in a way I had not seen before.

"You're a very attractive girl," he leered. "And talented, too." He grasped my hand, giving it a gentle kiss.

"Mr. Ceasare," I demurred, retrieving my hand. But the look was still there. "You're beautiful!" He leaned his face toward mine. My heart jumped to my throat as he came toward me, following me around the coffee table piled high with music.

"Mr. Ceasare, please leave me alone!" I threw my violin in its case, grabbed my music, and flew to my car. After this experience, I was reluctant to go for another lesson, but after a call from my mother, Mr. Ceasare behaved.

When I had moved to Richmond, and to a high school, I needed to prove to myself that I could fit in. I decided to investigate the other world of the popular crowd. I began to lead a double life: a high school sorority girl by day, a violinist at night.

Through my covert violin activities, I met the concertmaster of the University of Richmond Chamber Orchestra. William was eighteen and a senior, with wavy auburn hair, clear brown eyes and ruddy, sculpted cheekbones. I was smitten from our first meeting; only how could I, a mere sophomore, get him to notice me from my position far in the back as the last stand, second violin? I packed up my violin slowly after each rehearsal and lingered at my car. William was always the last one to emerge from the Gothic building.

Each time I initiated a conversation he was slow to respond. Then, just as I decided to give up, he asked me out. In a few months, Wayne became my first love. We shared our violin skills and our Southern Baptist background. Our favorite piece was the Bach Double Concerto. I was thrilled to share great music with someone I cared for, and happy to oblige when we were asked to perform for the youth group at his church.

William's mother looked exactly like June Billingsley, Beaver Cleaver's mother from the popular television show, *Leave it to Beaver*. Like the Cleavers, his family never argued. I envied him. I came from a family where differences of opinion were frequently expressed. When William escorted me to the Senior Prom, I was able to integrate the two parts of myself—the violinist and the popular sorority sister.

In 1969 I finished high school and got a scholarship to major in Violin at East Carolina University, leaving William in Richmond. On my first day, disoriented but excited, I descended the marble stairs in the Music Department main hall. Bordered by glass on all sides, practice rooms and professors' studios overlooked the lobby. Reaching the main floor, I heard a booming voice.

"Hey, Marilyn, wait up!"

A man of medium height waved to me. Thick black glasses framed his small brown eyes. Black hair dipped lazily over one eye. He wore a yellow shirt with a button-down collar and brown wing-tipped shoes with thick soles. His belly hung over his pants and I glimpsed a white tee shirt underneath.

"Yes?"

"Do you remember me?"

"Sure." I laughed. "You're the one who's responsible for me being here!"

"You've got that right. I am Fred Hall. My dad jammed with your mom in Richmond."

"Oh, yeah. I remember now. He played the banjo. And you came over, too, didn't you?"

"I did. That's when I told you about E.C.U."

"Hey, by the way, my fraternity is having a party tonight. Would you like to go?"

"Sure, why not."

"Pick you up at six."

"Okay." With a nervous gesture, Fred flipped his hair over his forehead. I observed him more closely. His nose was crooked, his lips thin. I was not particularly attracted to him, but he was determined to go out with me. I was a naive freshman, too polite to resist him. And I was flattered by the attention of an upperclassman. Fred played the snare drums. He performed in the marching band. At football games, I cheered him on prancing across the field at half time. He looked good in his red, white and gold uniform.

Becoming an accomplished violinist required every resource I had. Many extra hours of practice were necessary in addition to my regular curriculum. I arrived at the Music Building at six a.m. every day to practice for a few hours before my first class, usually functioning on four hours of sleep a night. Dr. Paul Q. Topper, my violin teacher, was tough, stern and exacting. Though I put in six hours of practice a day in addition to my regular curriculum, I often left my lesson brimming with tears. Fortunately, Dr. Topper tempered his criticism with love.

Fred was very persistent. He had set his sights on me and would not let me go. From that first day, he courted me without ceasing. One evening he arranged for his fraternity to serenade us in front of my dormitory. I was flattered that he regarded me as his sweetheart, and it was obvious that he adored me. On that night, he asked me to marry him. I did not know what to say. He was not particularly attractive or imaginative, but he was loyal. Without much thought I accepted, feeling guilty about William. He still sent a love letter from Richmond daily. Finally, my conscience would not allow the duplicity to continue. On a visit to my parents, I told him.

"William, I'm afraid I have some bad news," I began.

"Yes?" he said expectantly.

I was so sorry I had to do this. "I'm seeing someone else." I could not bear to tell him the whole truth.

"Oh," he muttered. "Well, I guess that's it, then. I'd better go." He turned and slammed the front door. I felt a crushing guilt. How could I be so heartless? Nevertheless, Fred was so insistent—and he was a part of my new life, not the old.

After my sophomore year, I decided to attend summer school. From my first lesson with Dr. Topper, I learned that I had a lot of catching up to do. There were violin virtuosos who had had more training at an earlier age than I had. My lack of experience gave me an added incentive. I signed up for summer school, vowing that nothing could stop me from succeeding at the violin. Before the session began, I visited Richmond, where a dental examination revealed that my wisdom teeth were growing incorrectly. The surgeon suggested that I have all four pulled.

"It's a routine procedure," he said to my mother. "She'll be home in a few hours. A hospital stay is completely unnecessary."

"If you insist, Doctor." Mother was not convinced that such a major procedure without the benefit of hospital facilities was wise.

Even so, the operation went smoothly. When the anesthesia wore off, I went home with sulfa drugs to prevent infection. On the way home, bleeding and traumatized I sat in the car as Mother ran errands. Soon I recovered and returned to college for the summer session.

One morning I took the violin out of its case. Enlarged and swollen, the middle joints of my second and third finger of my left hand barely moved. The next day this distressing condition had spread to the ball of my right foot. This bump was hard and sore, painful to stand on. I was hoping that this was a small incident, but I did not want to alarm my family, so I decided to consult a specialist on my own. From the confusing medical terminology in the yellow pages I selected the listing for an internist and made an appointment.

Afternoon sun streamed through the courtyard behind him as the physician took a cursory look at my swollen hands. "You have rheumatoid arthritis," he glanced up. "You are a good candidate for gold shots."

"How can you be sure?"

"Nothing in medicine is certain." His voice carried a hint of condescension. "But this treatment has a good prognosis for rheumatoid sufferers."

I was shattered and incredulous. My fate was ordained because of this brief examination? The joints of rheumatoid arthritis sufferers often swelled to twice the normal size. My fingers would become gnarled barnacles. Violin playing would be impossible. Tears streamed down my face as the doctor continued his explanation, oblivious to my emotional state.

No, I thought. I cannot accept this diagnosis. "Thank you for your time," I mumbled as I bolted from the office. Safe in the front seat of my car, I sobbed until there were no more tears. For the first time in my life, I felt utterly alone. I dried my eyes, ran to a telephone and dialed my mother.

"Mom, this can't be true!" I cried.

"Don't cry, Marilyn," she said. There was comfort in her voice. "Come to Richmond. See Dr. Toone. We will find out the truth. I doubt that you have rheumatoid arthritis. He takes one look at you and decides you have arthritis? Let us test you at the Medical College of Virginia. I hope you don't have anything, but if you do you'll need a better opinion."

"Couldn't I ignore it? Maybe it'll go away."

"It's more likely that it will get worse, darling. Wouldn't you like to know what caused the swelling?"

"I guess so. I'll come next week."

I sorted through my emotions. I told myself, This is just a bad dream. I will find out I am healthy and I can forget this ever happened.

Dr. Elias Toone was Mother's doctor, a renowned lupus specialist. Mother often sought his advice. She had implicit faith in his ability to heal her.

With my new perspective, I took a second look at the events that had occurred before I left home. Enveloped in my own concerns, I had hardly noticed that Mother's health was slipping. Now I acknowledged the fears I had pushed aside. Indeed, during my recent visits Mother always seemed to be emerging from a flare. Without acknowledging the reality of my mother's condition, I had watched the corners of her life slowly narrow. She seemed helpless against the strange power of the disease. Moreover, I sadly realized that lupus had already been part of my life for many years. Now I must deal with its reality in myself.

I struggled to grasp this development. There was no cure for lupus. Mother had followed her doctor's advice without question, at times succumbing to a panic which worsened her condition. Observing her, I vowed not to let the disease dictate my choices. I had given my consent and had to follow through, but I was terrified at the possible outcome.

Though inheritance of the condition was rare, doctors were intrigued at the possibility that I might have lupus as well as my mother. My tests at the Medical College of Virginia were informal. Rather than visiting a sterile laboratory, I settled into an outpatient suite overlooking the streets of downtown Richmond. The suite was tangerine and gold with a comfortable couch that doubled as a bed. During my free time, I made telephone calls. I went shopping. After three days, based on genetic proclivity and a few LE (lupus erythematosus) cells spotted in a blood test, Dr. Toone diagnosed lupus. I was relieved to be free of the taint of rheumatoid arthritis—a disease of useless, swollen joints which would surely end my violin career—but alarmed to lay claim to my Mother's fate of rashes, anemia and fevers. Her suffering would be a mirror for my own.

Though I was not ready to accept it, the diagnosis would affect everyone around me. After I telephoned my fiancée, a few hours passed. Fred had called his mother, a medical technician, to ask her advice.

"Marilyn, I'm afraid," he began.

"So am I, Fred."

"Mom says that the lupus patients she has seen were all terminally ill. She told me that lupus victims face a future of invalidism. The wedding should be called off, she told me…" his voice dropped off uncertainly.

My heart stopped. This was frightening news. Mother's bouts with lupus had been relatively mild. This reaction seemed a little exaggerated. So Mrs. Hall didn't want her precious son consorting with an invalid! I had never felt so hurt, humiliated and frightened. Would this really be my future?

"Look, Fred," I began. "Whether you choose to marry me or not is up to you. However, I think your mother is painting an unrealistic picture. My mother has had lupus for eleven years and nothing major has happened to her. I just can't believe I would end up as"—I choked on the words—"an invalid."

Fred was crying. "I know, Marilyn, but my mother…"

"Think about it, Fred, and let me know," I said, suddenly angered by his indecision. I hung up. After my tests were completed, I escaped to my parents, who provided a temporary cushion from my new status. It was tempting to accept Mrs. Hall's predictions. Dad never mentioned it, but I sensed his concern. His favorite females were stricken with an identical, unpredictable disease.

Mother was angry. "I'm going to sue that dentist," she fumed. "It was his incompetence that initiated the flare. He insisted that you have all four teeth out at once, in his office! We should have insisted on hospitalization, or at least having one or two wisdom teeth removed at a time." Knowing that the lupus process, once begun, was difficult to reverse, she was trying to protect me.

Just after my diagnosis, Mother and I attended a lupus group in Richmond. Sensing the despair and frustration of those around me increased my panic and denial. The people in the group shared a set of beliefs that I could not embrace. I was determined to avoid sliding into a tacit acceptance of the disease and its symptoms as real. Therefore, I stayed away partly out of willfulness, partly out of fear, partly for self-protection.

Overnight the dynamics between me and my family changed. Expectations from each of the four varied according to their beliefs. Mom was certain that her struggles with lupus awaited me. Dad was afraid that I could not finish my education. Bob and Jeff, my younger brothers, treated me with a new regard. They assumed that Mother's bouts with the disease, her moodiness caused by prednisone, her frequent trips to the doctor, her butterfly rash and fevers, would become my own. As my brothers grew older and got into adolescent scrapes, Mother could be critical, particularly with Bob. After high school he lived at home and played in a rock band as a drummer. She did not approve of his lifestyle and was never shy about letting him know how she felt. It was possible that she was disappointed he had not gone to college. Bob, the middle child, was always a rebel. This often pitted him against Mother, since they were home together much of the time.

I sensed these unspoken emotions in my family and they confused me. I could not decide for myself how to react. Was I to embrace this disease, to think of it as 'mine'? Should I define myself in terms of it? If so, should I limit my activity? I did not know if my mother had asked herself these questions when she learned of her disease. I knew that, sometime during the eleven years since, she seemed to have accepted the disease and embraced it as 'hers'. I found this impossible to do. Lupus was not 'mine'. It was an aberration, a distortion of the normal function of the body.

I returned to college taking a small dose of cortisone as prescribed. Fred had decided that the risk was worth it and we began to plan our wedding. When my family had moved to Richmond, we had again joined a Baptist church nearby. Our wedding would be there. It would be formal, we decided. I would have a long white dress and bridesmaids.

As Dr. Toone advised, I rested. Nevertheless, I kept this new information away from my roommates. I was ashamed; afraid the diagnosis would affect my standing at school. Following my mother's example, I took the discomfort in stride and after a few weeks, the swelling subsided.

I called Mother more frequently than before the diagnosis. The disease brought us even closer. Yet, whereas Mother had decided that having lupus was a point of honor, I was ashamed. I fought the accepted belief that the disease was real. To me it seemed an illusion, a temporary blindness. I felt that I should be able to eradicate it by unearthing its cause. I had no idea how this might be accomplished, but I vowed that lupus would never be more than a footnote in my life. I would never allow it to take center stage.

IV.

Discoveries

By the age of nineteen I wore the stigma of a chronic disease, one which might get worse with time and could possibly be fatal. Flannery O'Connor, the author who ultimately succumbed to lupus, once said, "I have never been anywhere but sick. In a sense, sickness is a place more instructive than a long trip to Europe, and it's always a place where there's no company, where nobody can follow."

Though the first flare was mild, I feared for the future. If I submitted to lupus, my career was over before it started. I had to protect myself. My survival was at stake.

My brother Bob had developed rheumatic fever as a child. My cousin Teresa had found some LE cells in a blood test, though the doctors had not made an official diagnosis. In our family, a weakness for rheumatic diseases was evident.

There was no 'cure' for this strange disease. Supposed 'management' was only possible with toxic drugs. I raged at the label 'lupus erythematosus', and at the mandate to take cortisone with its harmful side effects. I simply refused to accept that I 'had' the disease. Yet, after consulting with the doctors and my mother, I came to the sad conclusion that taking cortisone and facing the consequences was to be my fate.

My vision of music as a transcendent force had led me to play the violin, but concert violinists need strong constitutions. If the world of medicine to which I had turned offered an unsatisfactory solution, I would seek answers from a higher power. The medical journals suggested that emotional and physical stress were often catalysts in the worsening of the disease. In a painful evaluation, I would search my soul, examining the events leading to its first manifestation.

I was a sophomore in college. For the first two years at East Carolina I never missed a class of my academic schedule and practiced violin at least four hours a day. I probably had my first symptoms because of stress, sleep deprivation and the sulfa drugs I took after the wisdom teeth surgery.

The summer of my initial episode passed. A low dose of prednisone eased the swelling in my fingers. The joint pain became sporadic, then nonexistent. I was able to get on with my life.

It was exhilarating to leave my parents' home. The Sixties had changed the way we lived—from the dress code to experiments with drugs and alcohol. Bill and Wormy were friends of Fred's. They rented their own home where the parties were legendary. Wormy, a fine arts major, was an albino. He was rail-thin and sported a white Afro. His brother Bill was French major. We played records of the band *Chicago*, drank and partied. One evening I went into the kitchen looking for beer. Roaches scattered all over the filthy kitchen as the light illuminated their activities. It was exciting to share our new freedom. I reveled in the strange characters I met, so different from the people I knew during my sheltered upbringing.

At school, I developed a rivalry with Nancy Sanders, a talented violinist who was a junior. Poised and confident, she had a beautiful sound and a solid technique. I practiced diligently to catch up with her. I felt it imperative to surpass her by winning the concertmaster position of the school orchestra. Our rivalry drove me to work harder. Finally, I won the seat. Soon afterwards she switched to viola and left school. I felt guilty, though I knew this was an exaggerated response. I had validated my ambitions and proven myself a winner. Once I became concertmaster, I could imagine a future as a violinist. It was the first step on a long road, giving me confidence to proceed. My practice was finally showing results.

Fred and I married in November of my junior year. I had borrowed my cousin Donna's white gown. Although I wore a hand-me-down, I felt beautiful nonetheless as I waited at the back of our church for the cue to begin my walk up the aisle with Dad. While checking to see if we were starting on the correct foot, he glanced at me. "It'll never last," he declared, as *Here Comes the Bride* claimed our attention.

Though at the time I thought Dad was being cruel, he was right. Fred had definite expectations about his wife that were not at all what I wanted my life to be. After my victory over Nancy I had gained enough confidence to audition for a professional symphony, desperately needing to prove that I could make it in this highly competitive field. I had met with decent success, garnering several symphony offers across the country. I needed to prove to myself that I could make it on my own. This did not fit with Fred's expectations. He wanted me to stay at home and have children. Following me to the city of my job was out of the question. By the time I obtained my coveted degree in violin performance, I had already decided it would not work out. I had married too young. I felt terrible and knew that I was hurting him deeply, but there was no compromise and therefore no solution.

I was considering these various offers when I attended the Eastern Music Festival, a summer festival with a professional orchestra in residence in Greensboro, North Carolina. For our first concert, we were to play Mahler's *Fifth Symphony*. As a neophyte, I occupied the last chair and I prepared my second violin part carefully. Working with my first professional ensemble was an unparalleled experience. No recording could compete with the breadth of sound emanating from this huge orchestra. As a single thread in this tapestry of sound, I was participating in a glorious event beyond my wildest imaginings. It gave reality to my earlier celestial vision. Now I realized that, indeed, this world existed through the vehicle of great music.

At the same time, I enjoyed a new camaraderie with other musicians. Here I belonged to a community where all were conversant in the sublime language of music. I felt lifted off the surface of the earth through this perfect world which bypassed words and entered the soul directly.

When I mentioned to some violinists that I would like to work overseas, they gave me a list of orchestras with vacant positions. After the Festival, I returned to my parents' home. Armed with my degree I felt new self-reliance, new courage. Now it was necessary to carve a niche in the world of music. My audition success had given me the courage to explore every opportunity, so I made a tape of my senior recital and sent it to several orchestras abroad.

While awaiting the results, I worked as a waitress. Mother bought me several short costumes "for better tips". It was grueling. The strain of many hours standing caused the ball of my right foot to swell again. I enjoyed meeting my co-workers, but my heart remained with the violin.

During this break from playing, I decided to remove the shoulder rest, a bar that fits under the violin. I felt that the contraption inhibited the vibrations of the wood. My idol, Jascha Heifetz, played without one. I "weaned" myself, starting at the beginning. At first, I could not even play a scale. It was so discouraging that I cried after each session. Nevertheless, after weeks of dogged practice I finally broke through. With my new position, I felt freer than ever before. At the end of September, a telegram arrived. It was from the Iceland Symphony, inviting me to join their first violin section! Without a backward glance I packed my trunk and caught the first plane to Reykjavik.

My professional life had begun. Though at first I experienced culture shock, everything about this exotic country intrigued me. Our first tour with the Iceland Symphony began in a tiny village called, appropriately, Miniborg. The program was the *Polivetsian Dances* by Borodin, the Mozart *Piano Concerto Number Seventeen*, and Beethoven's *Fifth Symphony*. I found myself sitting with the concertmaster while the great pianist Vladimir Ashkenazy was playing and conducting just inches away! Mr. Ashkenazy glanced at us as he was conducting the Beethoven Fifth. "It's so much easier on the piano!" he said ruefully. We laughed at his admission. The music and the profound nature of Ashkenazy's artistry thrilled me.

Iceland was a fantastic country. I enjoyed the harsh climate and found that isolation agreed with me. I walked to and from rehearsals, braving the brutal wind barreling over the Cathedral at the top of the hill. Leifsgata, the street near my home, had small white houses topped with colorful roofs. I lodged with the family of a bassoonist in the orchestra and attempted to learn Icelandic. At my first pronunciation slip, the Icelanders would break into English. Because the island is isolated, the natives maintain the purity of their language, which resembles Latin and is virtually unchanged since Viking times. All Icelanders speak Icelandic, English and Danish with varying degrees of proficiency. Nordic linguists study the sagas—tales that are the folklore of the Icelandic people—to enhance their understanding of pure Icelandic.

Though other Americans in the orchestra missed their families back home, I gravitated to the environment. The other two Americans, cellists, were friends. Soon it would be my birthday. I wanted to have a spaghetti dinner with ground beef, but Icelanders only ate lamb. My friends searched downtown Reykjavik for ground lamb and made me a fabulous spaghetti dinner. Alone and in a strange country, it was comforting to know that my new colleagues cared.

Always aware of the lupus threat, I felt it necessary to get exercise. To increase my circulation I swam in pools heated by natural hot springs after our daily rehearsals at the Haskolabio, the local concert hall that was also a movie theater. Like the Icelanders I ran across the sheet of ice in my bikini and soaked in the hot tub. Then I negotiated the icy lining on the concrete walkway, swam my laps, and splashed into the hot tub. The hot and cold contrast had a bracing effect on my circulation.

I had arrived at the beginning of October, just after the symphony season began. Rehearsals began at nine-thirty. Each day I trudged through the park that ran through the center of Reykjavik. At my feet was pure white snow. Overhead the pitch-black sky set the white clouds off to perfection. After our rehearsal ended at noon I luxuriated in the premature sunset stretched over the park—it seemed designed just for me. Here the sky's brilliance displayed itself without the intrusion of Reykjavik's scrubby trees. Cottony clouds held center stage amidst a navy sky. The stars, like bits of diamond dust, sprinkled across the firmament. On several occasions, there was a display of the Northern Lights. In brilliant hues of green and pink, they danced across the entire blackened sky from horizon to horizon. It was a visual symphony, orchestrated to nature's perfect cadence.

I soon realized that I would always be a foreigner among the cordial Icelanders. The Americans in the military at Keflavik, a small town 35 minutes away from Reykjavik, knew nothing of my sense of proximity yet frustration. In their miniature United States they were marking time, not joining in the culture as I was.

Michael was a surgeon stationed in the Air Force. Handsome and athletic, he loved music and admired musicians. After we met at a subscription concert, our relationship progressed quickly. We planned a romantic skiing vacation in Akurerei, a picturesque town in the north. Though I had never been on skis, Michael assured me that it was easy.

"Just lean into the skis and snowplow to stop. Anyone can do it!" His enthusiasm was contagious, though I lacked his conviction. I made one successful trip down the intermediate slope with Michael by my side. There were no beginner slopes. Flushed with excitement and encouraged by my success, I took the lift up the mountain to the top of the intermediate slope. Michael continued to the advanced slope. Suddenly I lost my nerve. What was I doing here? I faced a steep incline which seemed beyond my capacity to slide down, realizing that I would stay right there until I could summon the courage to complete what I had started. Squaring my shoulders, I decided to go for it. Immediately I knew I had made a mistake. Icelandic toddlers whizzed by me as I careened down the hill, trying to lean forward, while knowing that this plummeting descent was the last thing I wanted to do. The sudden speed blinded me to any option other than stopping. I tried to snowplow, but I was going too fast and my bindings would not release. My right leg buckled under. I heard a sickening crack, then lost consciousness. The rescue workers found me in shock, set an inflatable raft around my leg, and spirited me down the mountain on a sled.

Michael was with them. He had been skiing above when a skier yelled, "Someone's broken their leg!" He whisked down to offer medical assistance and found that the person there—in shock—was his companion. At the rescue station, there were no facilities to set broken legs. "We'll take you to the hospital where we will put a cast on your leg," an Icelandic orderly informed me.

"I think we'll wait until we get back to Reykjavik," Michael interjected.

"The plane to Reykjavik doesn't come for three days," the orderly protested. "Miss Gibson should have her leg immobilized immediately!"

"I know, but she'll be okay until we get her there where she'll get better attention."

"Are you sure?"

"Believe me, she will be better off."

"All right. We'll admit her to the hospital until then."

After he left, still coming out of shock, I looked to Michael. "Why are you doing this, Michael? I need a cast now."

"These socialized medicine people are incompetent. Let me take you to Keflavik where my friend will put on a better cast. You will thank me for this. Your leg will heal correctly. Don't take a chance, Marilyn."

"All right, Michael. I trust you," I said, and blacked out again.

I awakened to a Siberian landscape of snowdrifts and fierce blizzard winds. Outside my window a lonely line of telephone poles stretched to infinity. After I registered in the small hospital, Michael vanished. I do not know where he went. Wistfully I watched him disappear, a lonely figure receding down the steep hill into town.

No one spoke English. I learned to say, "I am having very much pain" in Icelandic. However, the Icelanders in the northern part of the island did not approve of overmedication. Without an ability to communicate and pain as my lone companion, I longed for home.

The agonies that dominated my awareness, however, were difficult to ignore. So I detached from my body, marveling at the infinite and exquisite variation of pain. Piercing stabs alternated with excruciating stings, almost as if another body was experiencing all of it. Distancing myself from reactions of fear and avoidance I found, to my surprise, that the same finite laws as pleasure governed this pain. Separating the emotional factors had allowed me to categorize the pain. At times, the sensation, almost an electric impulse, came unbidden across the threshold of my feeling nature. Without the benefit of an emotional value judgment, such as, "This is pain; I don't want it", I was able to allow it to open my ability to experience sensation.

This discovery was a profound initiation, an insight I would remember in the years to come. It would become a tool in my understanding of disease.

After three torturous days, I flew back to Keflavik in a contraption that barely supported my broken leg. Michael's friend Karl plastered a full-length, twenty-pound non-walking cast over my entire right leg. Michael, aware of the lupus, monitored my bloodwork. I was not in touch with my doctor in the states. However, the small dose of prednisone that I was taking prevented fast healing of the spiral fracture. Instead of being in a cast for two months, I was in for four.

I took a two-week leave from the orchestra. Karl, a military resident, graciously offered his home in officer's housing. From my upstairs bedroom I listened to their two-year-old's tantrums, read Carl Jung, and ate baloney sandwiches. After two weeks of this experience, however, I was anxious to return to work. I arranged to stay with another family next door to the Haskolabio—a Scottish violinist named Bob, his wife and their two children. His dialect enlivened the many tales he told. I practiced in my small bedroom and prepared for a recital for the United States Information Service.

Although I was returning prematurely, after the two-week leave I resumed my job. Bob, the generous Scot, helped me crutch to rehearsals. Fortunately, my long black dress partially concealed the cast. I was thrilled to be working with Karsten Andersen, conductor of the Bergen Symphony of Norway. Maestro Andersen brought out the fierce, taut lines of Beethoven's *Eroica Symphony*. It was an exciting and virile performance. As a violinist himself, Andersen understood our approach to the music. He evaluated the scores from the first violinist's standpoint—with our melodic and bowing considerations. Andersen was an accomplished master whose understanding influenced me profoundly.

The state-supported Iceland Symphony supplied my medical care. My broken leg had cost 200 Kronur, the equivalent of two dollars! In addition, the care was commensurate to what I had received on the base. Shortly after Christmas, I had moved across town to a garret apartment on a street named Mavahlid. My attic rooms required that I negotiate the steps with crutches. After making it to the top, I was not able to crutch down until the next day. Here I forged a spiritual discipline along with a new relationship with myself. Michael returned to Los Angeles and a new position. Nancy Shook and Judy Serkin, the two American cellists, left in March. By the spring, I was alone from the end of our morning rehearsal until the next day. These solitary hours loomed parched and dry, waiting to be filled. It required a force of will to drag myself away from depressing thoughts, but the stereo and my tapes were fine companions. I slaked my thirst for spiritual fulfillment by listening to the masterworks—Mahler, Tchaikovsky, and Brahms. Isolation brought a raw awareness, a visceral knowledge that had never been possible before.

Winter melted into spring. After months of scarce sunlight, I relished the midnight sun traveling just above the horizon. The earth seemed covered with a golden aura that beckoned to us twenty-four hours a day. I loved watching Icelanders garden at two a.m. We were celebrating our emergence from the darkness and no one wanted to miss it.

The amber light sifted through my garret window almost twenty-four hours a day now. Like most Icelanders, I could not sleep. From my tiny window, I watched the gardeners and the children playing on the street. I made a covenant to practice six hours each day. I was physically unable to climb, so I would scale another type of mountain; the Bach solo sonatas. He wrote six unaccompanied works altogether. I vowed to use this opportunity to learn them all. Bach was my best companion through the secluded months before I returned to the States.

I recorded the Schumann Sonata for the Iceland National Radio. This brooding piece explores Schumann's whimsical side with a touch of dark fantasy. Gudrun, my Icelandic pianist, invited me to rehearse in her small, immaculate apartment. Afterwards she offered me Icelandic cakes. I was still limping. She also limped; one leg was slightly shorter than the other was. I wondered if she, too, felt isolated on this island of snow and ice.

I was proud to be a cultural emissary for the United States but I missed my native land. Though the orchestra asked me to stay for another season, I declined. It was time to go home.

Now deciding to attend the Aspen Music Festival, I reluctantly bid farewell to the country that had enabled me to take my first steps down the corridors of self-discovery.

V.

Journeys of Faith

I set out for Colorado. My flight to Aspen was spectacular. I could almost reach out and touch the snow-capped Rocky Mountains. Though I almost lost my breakfast, the first sight of these peaks was more than compensation for a little queasiness.

I had come to the Aspen Music Festival on scholarship. The Continental Inn, my assigned lodging, was a dormitory for music students by summer, a ski resort during their peak season. Constructed of rugged rock, it was a stark contrast to the small, colorful Icelandic dwellings. The West was an exciting change from Iceland's harsh climate. In those days, Aspen was still a cow town. I imagined horses tied to wooden rails on the dirt road called Main Street. I was a student again, ready for anything. One night I went dancing with some girlfriends at The Paramount, although I still had a limp. This fanciful club in turn-of-the century style contained wealthy ranchers who wore cowboy hats and had long, lean legs.

Margie Deutsch, my roommate, was a conducting student from Long Island. I admired her courage in attempting to succeed in a man's field. We got along well though she was working all the time. Her study required visits to the music department on the outskirts of town, so I was able to practice in our room alone. I continued the regimen I had begun in Iceland.

One night I was playing through the second movement of the Dvorak Concerto. I put my violin down to get a glass of water and the music continued exactly where I had stopped! I walked out on my balcony to investigate. Shlomo Mintz, the famous violinist, was laughing at the joke he had played. I laughed too; glad to discover I had not gone crazy. Shlomo had just arrived from Russia as a protégé of Isaac Stern. The next day I got a call from Francis, an employee of the festival.

"Marilyn, Shlomo would like to go out with you. I'll pick you up at eight."

That evening Francis arrived with Shlomo. We went to the Great Gorge for an ice cream sundae. It was strange going out with a chaperone, but Shlomo was a little young for me. What was interesting was the advice he had gotten from Mr. Stern, which was to practice constantly.

It was 1974 and I was twenty-three. At Aspen, I met many musicians from California who were interested in eastern philosophies. Living in North Carolina and then Iceland had isolated me from changes initiated in the early Seventies. I was surprised now to meet musicians who were transformed by these new ways of thinking.

I was still taking five milligrams of cortisone every other day. Though lupus was not active, it could surface at any time. Now, in this new atmosphere, I learned about natural alternatives to toxic drugs. I discovered yoga, became a vegetarian, simplifying my diet to steamed vegetables and brown rice, and continued my quest to rid myself of illness and seek spiritual solutions. I was to embrace selected ideals from this new counterculture that would open my mind to new possibilities.

Martin Able, a violist from California, embodied many of these principles, and introduced me to some appealing concepts. He was just a bit taller than I was, with reddish hair, a long, flat nose, and smiling blue eyes. He liked to stroke his beard in thoughtful moments.

I met him outside the registration building. Here, in the middle of the school, was a placid pond teeming with fish. This wooden edifice arched over the pond and housed our auditions, master classes and orchestra rehearsals. He was wearing a faded pair of corduroy jeans, beat-up tennis shoes and a rope for a belt.

"Who are you studying with?" he asked me.

"Fredell Lack," I replied. "She's great."

"How about you?"

"Lillian Fuchs."

"Wow," I said. Fuchs had a reputation as an excellent violist and a great teacher. "Where are you staying?"

"In a tent up there on that hill," he pointed. I was impressed. Camping on the school grounds was not allowed. After this beginning, Martin showed me in other ways that he enjoyed flaunting conventions. He was an avid conservationist and well acquainted with beautiful spots in the Southwest. He taught me to listen for voices in the white-water and spirits on the summits, as well as the names of mountain wildflowers and of the creatures named conies that screeched as they scurried across sun-dappled rocks.

One night five of us piled into a car bound for the Donner Pass, thirteen thousand feet above sea level. We scrambled over some granite boulders, and all at once, we were standing on top of the world. The sky, scattered with millions of glittering stars, clung to us like a blanket and for a brief, intoxicating moment, I became one of them. Star-born I spoke a familiar language, one that felt more comfortable than the human cloak I had temporarily discarded.

On another occasion, three of us piled into Kathy's blue Beetle for a ride to Vale. A Bach Brandenburg Concerto played in the cassette as each vista became more breathtaking than the last. The undulating rhythm of the music captured the living spirit of the earth. Bach had created this glorious music, a profound law unto itself. Yet, it was also the perfect expression of God's timeless physical world.

The practice area was located just on the outskirts of town, at the aptly named Roaring Fork River, where I got my first look at whitewater's formidable power. Since there was competition for the space, I attempted to arrive early enough to reserve a frigid practice room. After the sun went down the rooms again became barely warm enough to play in. Dorothy Delay, the teacher of Itzhak Perlman and other great violinists, brought prodigies such as Nigel Kennedy from Juilliard.

As my first summer in Colorado ended, I was uncertain where I should continue my education. Fredell Lack, my violin teacher at the Aspen Festival, had been a prodigy and still maintained an active solo schedule. I studied the Bach E Major Partita with her. Her interpretation, warm and always seeking a lush, silvery tone, influenced my playing greatly. Fredell's technical advice and her thorough knowledge of the score were necessary guidance after my solo study in Iceland. She invited me to the University of Houston on a fellowship, but I was not ready to return to the South. Martin suggested we try New York. We decided to move in together as lovers. I declined Fredell's offer, wondering if I had made the wrong choice. However, when Martin left Aspen early in order to find an apartment and located one next door to the Manhattan School of Music, I knew that I had made the right decision.

I arrived in the big city completely intimidated. Nothing in my young life had prepared me for the number of diverse people I observed. The culture shock was more severe than in Iceland but gradually I began to find it fascinating. Grant's Tomb stretched high over the park across the street from our apartment on Claremont Avenue. I began jogging in Riverside Park. The first time I ran on the concrete tiles shaped like honeycombs, I made it from 116th down to 96th Street and back. The next day I had a curious pain in my lower leg muscles. I had gotten shin splints. After a two-week recovery period, I vowed not to run on concrete with incorrect shoes

We found a bread shop down the street with freshly baked wholewheat. Martin and I followed the diet recommended in *Food is Your Best Medicine* by Henry Beiler. Beiler advocated steamed vegetables and brown rice. I embraced this diet, reasoning that lupus would stay away if I maintained pure habits.

I had not decided which graduate school to attend. I will study the violin privately, I rationalized, deciding to cancel my audition at the Manhattan School of Music. However, on the day of the audition I found new courage. "What have I got to lose?" I said to Martin before I bravely walked the half-block to school.

I performed the Dvorak Concerto for the distinguished jury of violinists, leaving the audition uncertain how it had gone. Later that day I had a private audition with the orchestra conductor, Anton Coppola. He asked for *Don Juan* by Strauss, an excerpt that I knew completely. I felt I played well, but it was difficult to discern his reactions. I returned to my apartment disconsolate. "They probably hated me," I told Martin. "Oh, well. I can always go back to my waitress job in Richmond."

The next day I received an answer. The committee had given me a full scholarship and concertmaster of the orchestra! I could not believe it. My professional experience in Iceland had certainly paid off. I was thrilled.

My teacher, Paul Zukofsky, was a great violinist, though a little unorthodox. Somewhat pale, he had dark hair and brown eyes. He often smoked a cigar at my lessons, which took place in a small studio at the school. He taught double-stop (two notes played simultaneously) scales in intervals of fourths, fifths and sevenths, as well as the traditional thirds and sixths. I memorized my etudes and worked on fine aspects of technique, though I sometimes sensed that I disappointed him. The strain of working so hard as well as wondering if I was pleasing my teacher manifested itself as renewed joint swelling.

Although I was ready for this intense work, I was a bit naive. I did not realize that each performance was a learning experience that enabled me to inch to a higher level. There was a gap between the size of my goals and my ability to achieve, a gap made greater by my teacher's expectations. The small sores on my hands and sporadic joint pain now directly affected that which I wanted so desperately to master.

Nevertheless, the conservatory atmosphere was hospitable to my career ambitions. It had been the right decision. I continued my small dose of cortisone, although I was beginning to believe that the drug was full of side effects that would ultimately hinder me. Each visit with my mother strengthened my theories. Now she had rheumatoid arthritis as well as lupus, and the drugs did not hasten an end to these plagues. By the time I entered graduate work at the Manhattan School of Music, she was struggling with high blood pressure and heart problems.

Exercise was a vital part of my emerging self-management program. My father arose at dawn and jogged ten slow miles on my high school track. During my visits home I joined him. I attempted to persuade Mother to come along. However, her aching joints prevented her from getting started. Mother believed in the wisdom of doctors and their ability to heal through drugs. My faith in medical magic bullets had never been strong. Watching my mother gradually become disabled reinforced my skepticism. Prednisone could keep the disease at bay but not heal it. Its first legacy to me had been doubling the length of time it took for my leg to heal. I would soon discover that the destructive capabilities of the drug were even more extensive than I realized.

The sores on my hands and mild joint pain I had developed in my first quarter of graduate school suggested lupus activity. I was dismayed at this appearance of symptoms. Mr. Zukofsky suggested a physical therapist at the New York Hospital. The exercises came with a large bill. Entrepreneurial medical care was a shock after the humane system in Iceland. The exercises, designed for an arthritic, were not particularly helpful. At least in my case, lupus joint pain moved from one side of the body to the other. It never stayed long enough to become entrenched like arthritis. In spite of their ineffectual results, the treatments led me to believe that physical exercise is a necessity in the management of lupus. I noticed that the joint swelling subsided after jogging, reasoning that if lupus moves through the blood, increased circulation would decrease its activity. There was no medical support for my theory, but somehow I knew it was right. As I continued my self-imposed program, the joint pain gradually ceased. By the time I finished my graduate degree, I was free of pain and completely off cortisone. This achievement confirmed my theories.

I continued to seek answers to my disease from other sources. My first church was the Southern Baptist. I was descended from a line of ministers. My father was not as strict as many Baptists who forbade dancing and card playing, but he felt most comfortable in the atmosphere of his youth.

After my baptism at the age of eight I felt like a slate washed clean. Yet when the initial the initial thrill of being sinless faded I wondered how long I could maintain this glorious perfection before slipping back into the category of "worthless sinner".

In high school, a friend had introduced me to Ayn Rand and her doctrine of personal accomplishment as put forth in *Atlas Shrugged*. I experimented with this concept when I could not seem to summon the emotions my Baptist congregation felt at the call for commitment. While that Baptist belief in Jesus Christ taking responsibility for my sins was a wonderful concept, it seemed to divorce me from the imperative to change. My understanding at that time was that Christ was an intermediary between God and me. Because of this, however, my answer to the call for commitment felt false and I wondered if my belief was serving others or me.

I had begun more consciously to rebel after leaving my parents' home. Through my years in college, and later in Iceland, my artistic world seemed a substitute for religion. In trips across the country, and, particularly in the Southwest, I forged a new relationship with nature and its relevance to art. On a trip across the desert I found pieces of driftwood on which I fashioned elaborate wall hangings made of jute and macramé. They seemed to emerge from me fully formed. Now I practiced yoga before morning classes and taught myself the basic postures. Allan Watts, a Westerner who articulated these concepts for the Western mind, guided me.

After a year of yoga and vegetarianism, I began to recognize that I had certain psychic powers. On occasion, the thoughts of others were apparent to me. One evening I went to a party of eminent composers at a brownstone on the Upper West Side. I was making small talk with a well-known composer when, suddenly, I heard his thoughts in my head. They were sometimes words, and at other times emotional reactions to what others or I had said. It was as if I was able to take a slice of the person's life, almost as if I became that person. Emotional reactions that were very new to me floated through my awareness and almost possessed me. I had to disengage to keep the messages from coming. Most often, I knew people's devious thoughts. No one seemed to be genuine or caring. At least in the limited survey I made, the party guests seemed to be manipulating their friends for personal gain. Nevertheless, eavesdropping on these ugly inner landscapes felt wrong. I left the party shaken and frightened. It seemed I had stumbled on to a formidable skill, but I was not sure how to use it. Without tools to manage these feelings, I stopped practicing yoga, the very process that had brought me the beginnings of mind control and a profound peace. However, the loss that resulted left an empty void and I found myself searching for alternatives.

My first year of graduate school was over. Martin and I had parted. It seemed that, although he was a California hippie, he had control issues and an authority problem with his father. Living with him had become intolerable, so I found a summer sublet with Marcia, an oboist in Greenwich Village. Marcia was vivacious, entertaining and always ready for fun. We shared many things that summer, reveling in the free spirit of the Village in the Seventies. One day I discovered a metaphysical bookstore called The Mad Monk on Eighth Street. It was full of original pottery and spiritual books. On that day, a particular title seemed to leap out at me: *Concentration and Meditation* by Christmas Humphreys. I bought it immediately. On that scorched afternoon I bore the book home, ascended to my tar rooftop, set up a lounge chair, and reverently began to read. Mr. Humphreys, a British judge who had developed a passion for Buddhism, gave practical advice to Westerners beginning the practice. As a scholar who had attained a high level of accomplishment in meditation, he emphasized the goal of Enlightenment. His books provided a basic knowledge of the schools of Buddhism and their varying paths to Enlightenment.

The words of *Concentration and Meditation* seemed to leap off the page and beckon to me. I 'understood' certain concepts completely. It was as if I had pondered them for years, possibly lifetimes. I was enthralled to discover the religion that promised inner peace. Inadvertently I had stumbled onto the answers I had been seeking! I began to meditate in lotus posture. My acquaintance with yoga made this was a familiar process. *Concentration and Meditation* had given me the courage to jump directly into Zen meditation about nothingness, or 'the void'. My psychic powers were no longer an unwieldy vehicle. Now they were tools that would guide me through the abyss of strange supernatural occurrences. Through this book, I learned of the value of concentration. Moreover, I found that losing oneself in 'the void', or 'the silence', where the subconscious can be accessed, would be most successful when concentration is mastered. I learned to focus on simple items for longer and longer periods without allowing my mind to wander. This was not an easy task. I began with simple concentration exercises from *Concentration and Meditation*. Humphreys was adamant: "Meditation through the higher levels is unattainable without elementary mind control," he warned. With Enlightenment as my goal, I began the difficult task of stilling my mind. Each day I set aside a quiet time to connect with the source, or the God within. At first, I was unaccustomed to halting my thoughts. As I attempted to concentrate on mundane objects, a few minutes would pass while I wondered what was for supper or what I was going to do that evening. Then I would return to the rock I had chosen as my subject. After several weeks, I made some progress. Zen lore describes Masters who attained Enlightenment instantly. I knew these accomplishments were rare, and indeed, I was far from attaining this goal. However, I persevered, and in a matter of weeks, I was able to control thoughts in daily life. My mind had been like a radio station repeating the latest musical snippet I heard while shopping or my latest performance. I possessed this ability to retain sounds—I had a "phonographic memory" but sometimes I could not turn it off. Still, music may have been better than negative thoughts, and Humphreys suggested that a musical snippet is superior to negative words. However, mind chatter, or uncontrolled random thoughts, can interfere with the attainment of inner peace. Increasingly, through my new concentration practice, I was able to eliminate this mental interference.

After several weeks of concentration practice, I progressed to the next step. Counting exhalations up to ten is the soul of Zen. With a little bit of control, I found that I could stay with the count all the way to ten. If my mind wandered, I began again with one. Coming out of these sessions was like awakening from a profound sleep. I emerged with precious gems of knowledge culled from my inner source.

Soon after I began this practice, I began to develop the equanimity similar to that the Buddhists describe. My mind became calm, unfettered to past or future. In Sanskrit, the word *samadhi* refers to 'one pointedness', which means concentration on only one thought. In *samadhi* the swaying of a tree or the laugh of a child are joyous discoveries. A *satori*, or awakening, experience came to me straight away. It occurred during an afternoon meditation that was unremarkable in most respects. My meditation room was cool and dimly lit, sheltered from the sweltering sun. As I entered waking consciousness, I noticed my right hand as it moved across my field of vision. There were gauze-like tentacles in the shape of a spider web between each finger. This almost transparent shape shifted with each motion of my hand.

In this single moment it became evident that each act, no matter how insignificant, emanates ripples of circumstance. Nothing is inconsequential. Each motion, first a thought in my mind, then a manifest reality, creates other motions. As a spider weaves her web, each skein tightens its sphere of influence. Suddenly I awakened to the possibility that every action is bound to its cause. Each action, therefore, has far-reaching results. This knowledge could release me from suffering caused by actions without regard for the consequences.

My revelation led me to seek greater mind control. After my experience with *Concentration and Meditation,* I devoured all of Christmas Humphreys's books, where I learned that Buddhism is a solitary pursuit through the practice of meditation. "Life consists of suffering," the Buddha says, "unless you free yourself from the round of becoming, which is the karmic wheel of rebirth created by unfinished karma. One is only able to break free from facing his karma by gaining control over each action, each intent. The Buddhists believe that freeing yourself from desire will set you on your path toward Enlightenment. This process also involves facing karma created in this and past lives. Karma binds you to the earth. Karma exists through any negative emotion such as hatred, fear, anger, guilt, sorrow, or greed. Like my single motion of the hand, these reactions create webs of circumstance, which are as real as physical webs. All humans are entangled whether they are aware of it or not.

I pondered this new knowledge in meditation and conscious awareness. I could choose to use this revelation in daily life. This would require me to monitor my thoughts with great diligence to insure that I did not ensnare myself needlessly. It was a monumental task, thus to become aware of errant thoughts and weed them out. However, this vision was a guidance. I owed a debt of gratitude to those who had shown it to me.

I taught violin at the USDAN, a summer music camp on Long Island in this summer of 1975. The bus left from the Village early in the morning. I meditated before the school day began, using the bus trip for concentration practice. Through this discipline of blocking out background noise and clearing mental chatter, my mind became a placid pond.

After graduating from the Manhattan School, I used psychic awareness to locate a roommate. An ad in the *Times* noted an apartment on Ninety-ninth Street. I entered the lobby and walked down the narrow corridor to the small elevator. It was as if an invisible hand had pushed me inside and taken me to the eighth floor. The doors opened almost on signal and a petite woman with rosy cheeks, sandy hair, and an impish smile appeared across the hall, beckoning to me. Suzanne's sunny apartment was overflowing with plants. Shining parquet floors reflected the cheery decor. After a quick tour, I agreed to become her roommate. As I was leaving, I noticed a dingy second-floor apartment with the double doors open on my right. This was actually the apartment advertised in the *Times*! Amazed at my good fortune, I began a mutually beneficial relationship with Suzanne.

Suzanne, who played the guitar and sang folk songs with a lilting Irish contralto, was also a student of yoga. My Zen meditation practice was comfortable for her. She agreed that management of lupus was always an important consideration. With her encouragement, I became a zealous jogger, never missing a day. Afterwards I sweated in Suzanne's portable sauna. Soon the joint swelling was gone and lupus was in remission. Deciding that prednisone, even as a maintenance dose, was unwise, I stopped taking it. My mother's deterioration made me fearful of the power of the drug.

Slowly I would find more work playing the violin. However, until I could support myself playing, teaching would serve as an interim occupation. I got a job in Brooklyn Heights and taught in a community-sponsored a string program in the Bedford-Stuyvesant section. Here many young mothers were raising their babies alone. The spirit of these African-American people shone through the desolate landscape like the stars I had almost touched at Donner's Pass. I marveled at their resourcefulness, their strength. One frigid day I was sitting on a bus. A young mother climbed the steps clutching a small bundle. She paid her fare and settled into a front seat. Opening the child's hood, she revealed a perfect face with long lashes and beautiful brown eyes. She smiled down at him, flooding him with love. I felt a wave of compassion, or *karuna*, as the Buddhists call it. My Zen practice had shattered the scales of illusion. I felt the sweet adolescent mother's love as my own. I was the mother and the son simultaneously.

The Buddhists say, "Being is becoming and becoming is being". I was focusing increasingly on soaring through higher and higher realms of bliss, but not so much on becoming the best violinist that I could be. My first year out of school was not garnering much work playing the violin, but my meditation was gathering strength. The sensation was beyond joy. It was like being in a heaven. My creativity increased. I wrote prolific poetry. I wanted to explore every aspect of this new way of life. I even fantasized about entering a Japanese Zen monastery. From my first taste of Zen, I had imagined being in the monasteries of Kyoto. I wondered how a monastic life would make the attainment of Enlightenment, if not certain, at least a goal having fewer distractions.

I sorted through alternatives. Surely, awareness of higher realms was preferable to being a violinist in New York City. In contemplating such a move, I would be following a trend of East-West exchanges. Phillip Kapleau, an American who trained in Japan, was an inspiration. Shinichi Suzuki, a famous roshi, or teacher, had also attained Enlightenment and come to America to teach. These men had dedicated their lives to seeking Enlightenment.

Yet, the deciding factor in my decision to remain on my present career course was lack of desire. I had attained something like what the Buddha described. It was an abiding sense of bliss that was quite wonderful. Now there was little motivation to play the violin or search for work. Although the Buddha urged us to follow "The Middle Way", and not to leap into asceticism, denying one's physicality on earth, it was nonetheless tempting. Bypassing the difficulty involved in achieving my goals as a violinist, I could meditate instead.

Although I had never given up the violin, my primary focus had been meditating and practicing. In fact, my playing had improved since tapping into The Self. I was simply unaccustomed to the placid feeling after meditation that made everything all right and my goals framed with less emotion. I had gained so much from this wonderful religion and the beautiful example the Buddha set with his vow to bring "the last blade of grass" to Enlightenment. I wanted to find Enlightenment and dwell with the Boddhisatvas. Nevertheless, I would soon realize that my destiny lay in combining Eastern and Western approaches to forge a deeper understanding through my quest for truth.

From my glorious vision of the heavens revealed through the celestial music of the violin, my course had indeed been set. Must I not, still, follow that voice? Realizing that my lack of initiative could indicate an imbalance, I pulled back from a complete dedication to Zen. I gave up my fantasy to go to Japan and reduced my meditation time. Yet, Buddhist principles would remain a part of my life. Although I reluctantly shifted my entire focus away from Buddhism, it would continue to give me valuable insights.

VI.

Traveling to My Death

My Buddhist practice had cleared away the disturbance of uncontrolled thoughts. Free of conflicting emotions, I discovered a profound joy in living that manifested as normal health. I became increasingly active in a search for a better teaching situation, discovering the School for Strings, a Suzuki school in New York that fit my needs perfectly. After a two-year training program, I joined the faculty. I also accepted a job as Associate Professor at Long Island University.

Feeling ever more alive, I met David, a filmmaker. He was handsome, charismatic, and more established in his career than I. He had seemed unapproachable—almost a fantasy. Nevertheless, I could not seem to avoid him. I saw him at my favorite restaurant daily and often ran into him on the street. I thought my feelings had little impact. Then, one day, David sat down next to me.

"I noticed the book you were reading," he began, with a dark smile.

"Yes. Italo Calvino. I'd love to go to Italy someday."

"It's a wonderful place," he agreed. I was amazed when he asked me out for supper. Yet soon we were seeing each other regularly. David's seniority of fourteen years lent him an air of sophistication I lacked.

At first, our love was wildly romantic. We went to France for a romantic tryst, soaking up Paris as only lovers can. David wrote sublime poetry to celebrate our union. I was impressed by David and delighted in his creativity.

My free-lance performing career flourished as I gave solo recitals at Long Island University and played different kinds of music. David and I continued to see each other. After several years of this arrangement, I suggested to David that we make it legal. "If it's what you want, Marilyn," he said; though I sensed something in his voice that should have warned me.

After our marriage, we stopped communicating. The distance between us grew. Sadly, communication through poetry was our only joining. The effect of this stress had taken an alarming toll on my body. Slowly, imperceptibly, my skin turned yellow. I stopped eating regularly and my weight dropped twenty pounds. Finally, the tension between us escalated into a confrontation. David demanded an end to the marriage, even suggesting that I see a counselor. Hoping to salvage our relationship, I made an appointment with a woman downtown.

I arrived at the psychiatrist's office and attempted to relate my story but could only managed to sob uncontrollably. During our 45-minute session (for which she charged me $75), she informed me that my jaundiced skin indicated that I should be in a hospital instead of a therapist's office! I staggered to the street and summoned a cab to the nearest hospital emergency room. The doctors said that I was suffering from life-threatening hemolytic anemia. This is a lupus manifestation in which the body makes antibodies that attack its red blood cells.

The doctor ordered 100 milligrams of cortisone intravenously each day. My first megadose of steroids was a profound shock. Though I realized that this was a standard treatment, I was furious that I had to take it. It was an assault, a terrifying ride through the dark side. My mind raced helplessly around the clock. There were monstrous mood swings. I was in a mental straight jacket, yet my anemic body felt like a limp rag. Dr. Jack Hooker, my lupus specialist, discussed removing my spleen. I resisted his idea, and narrowly escaped with my organ intact. I could not believe this was happening to me. With an unreasoning, drug-induced anger, I denied the reality of my condition.

At the first sign of trouble, David had gone to Hollywood to make a film and he ceased all communications with me. Despite Dr. Hooker's recommendation that I stay, I left the hospital after only a week and before the anemia had been reversed. My decision was governed in part by financial concerns. I had absolutely no health insurance and David had deserted me. Fortunately, a helpful aide from the Manhattan School informed me that there was a foundation for graduates that might fund my bill. I applied and it was paid. This experience showed me that insurance was a necessity for the future.

Though I was free from the hospital and my steroid IV line, I was still yellow and anemic. I dragged myself about, unable to function without great effort. Again, I sought the solace of my parents' home where Mother was recovering from a heart attack. Fighting this latest setback as well as rheumatoid arthritis was difficult. She could not move without pain.

I, too, felt a deep malaise. My entire body rebelled at the effort required to stay alive, and each action required a strong will. At least now, I was home. I donned my pajamas and sank into the king-sized bed beside her. My father waited on us. During the day, while Dad worked at the Life of Virginia, we watched soap operas and commiserated about our conditions. Now that he was an executive Vice President of the company, I was sorry that he bore the responsibility for keeping our needs satisfied.

"I am glad you are here, Marl," Mother said, taking my hand and patting it. "How could David do this to my little girl! He wasn't your type, really." She raised her eyebrows, tiny lines of suffering creasing her forehead. "We'll take care of you and you'll be fine in no time; you'll see." She paused. "You shouldn't have left the hospital when you did, honey."

"But, Mom".

"It was for your own good. The doctors know what they're doing."

"I just couldn't stay. It was horrible," I said. I had anticipated her response and I wished that I could agree with her. She was more experienced in the effects of this horrible disease. Nevertheless, each flare-up that weakened her further brought a feeling of panic. Reentering the hospital seemed totally out of the question. Where was the hope for a healthy life? Yet, I did hold out for this hope, believing that, somehow, if I could achieve my health, I would find the key that would unlock the mystery of my body's defenses gone awry. Sharing the experience of lupus brought us together, but I could not accept my fate of being a lupus victim as if it was a badge of identity. Though I enjoyed the nurturing atmosphere at home, my mother's beliefs in medical treatments for a nonetheless insuperable disease stifled me. I was desperate to prove that I was right in seeking solutions elsewhere. Finding no support at home for my desire for alternative methods of healing, I became determined to begin a clandestine search on my own.

One Spring Sunday I put on an off-white jersey dress and high-heeled sandals. I drove through a rolling, verdant section of Richmond to a Christian Science service. Mary Baker Eddy taught healing through the love of Jesus Christ. I returned from the service inspired, realizing that healing must occur in the higher dimensions I had reached through my earlier meditative states. Following the example of Mrs. Eddy, I would bring my spirit upward. I hurried upstairs to my bedroom and relaxed my body, clearing my mind of emotions. I imagined that I was floating in the etheric world where a healing could take place.

It was too little too late. My meditative practice had slipped since our marriage. This lapse had exacerbated my emotional upheaval after it ended. Like playing the violin, thought control requires practice—and commitment. Meditation is still considered suspect by most Westerners. My husband did not meditate in a regular way, though he did use short periods of reflection and visualization before beginning a new film. I realized, through this attempt to cure myself, that a previous meditative practice may have allowed me to monitor the thoughts that had caused the illness. If I had kept it up I could have controlled these thoughts and the anemia might not have developed.

To reclaim the health I had lost, I returned to meditation vigorously. Healing tapes were helpful. They empowered me to relax and envision restoration. In my determination to dig myself out of this crisis with natural methods, I followed Adele Davis' strict diet of liver, which I hated. I decided that I would heal myself without prednisone. I stopped taking the twenty-milligram daily dosage prescribed by Dr. Hooker. I was aware that the shock from this withdrawal might have put me back in the hospital but was determined to prove that I could beat lupus.

My parents were alarmed. Dad was afraid my rebellion would worsen Mother's condition, so I decided to leave. Still jaundiced and functioning on half the normal number of red blood cells, I took the money from our marriage separation settlement and set off for my uncle's family reunion in Brewster. I attempted to join in the revelry with my relatives, but it seemed like I was walking underwater.

Next I flew to Aspen and stayed in a quaint little hotel called the Little Red Ski Haus, a favorite of music students, where many of my friends were staying. Like the student I had recently been, I attended string quartet master classes and went hiking. I pretended that I was normal, but I was living a lie. I was not a student. I was seriously ill, unable even to play the violin. I felt like an alien who had beamed down into paradise.

The next morning I encountered Martin. We caught up as he described his adventures in China and other exotic destinations. He was still eating natural foods and preserving the environment, playing in chamber music groups and orchestras. It was good to see him again but he was too self-involved to realize the extent of my dilemma. I looked normal except for my yellow caste. Besides, I did not want my friends to know the dire nature of my condition. As I took my leave of Martin, I met Vicki, a friend who was a Christian Scientist. We decided to hike the American Lake Trail, a strenuous uphill climb. I dragged along behind her, stopping for air at every switchback. It seemed I had overestimated my capabilities. Finally, through sheer effort of will, I made it to the lake. It had been well worth the effort. The gray curves of the Rockies sloped to the glassy surface of the lake, unspoiled and completely isolated. "This may be my last chance to see such a sight," I sighed. My condition was steadily worsening. If this downward spiral continued, I did not have much time left.

Running from the inevitable, I fled to San Diego. My friend Karla, a cellist in the San Diego Symphony, offered her airy apartment and helped me to purify my diet. San Diego was paradise. The climate was dry and sunny with perfect temperature year-round. Exotic plants grew everywhere. Fruits and vegetables were unlike anything in the East. Despite my efforts, I had become so ill that a trip to the store was pushing the limit of my capability. I still believed I could cure myself through purifying the toxins in my body. I would eat only organic fruits and vegetables, pure water and vitamins. One day we purchased some organic beets. Enthusiastically I made some juice, but I could not keep it down and discharged it in pink spurts all over Karla's bathroom. I was embarrassed, but Karla was a good-natured hostess and glossed over the incident.

One day we drove to Tijuana. I was thrilled to be in Mexico but afraid to drink or eat anything. The smells were nauseating to my weakened system. We passed a tortilla shop where the high-pitched sound of the ancient, oily tortilla machine made me queasy. I could not shake the feeling of separateness from healthy people. I was so vulnerable.

The San Diego Symphony season was beginning. Karla returned to work and gently suggested that I move. I investigated health spas in the desert, but my dwindling energy made it impossible to travel. So I checked into a motel near Pacific Beach. Each diet purification technique had left me weaker. I was running out of alternatives. I decided to try acupuncture. Since I was unable to negotiate public transportation, Karla drove me to the acupuncturist. After my treatments, I returned to my darkened hotel room alone. My diet had narrowed to distilled water, bananas and vitamins. Once a day I summoned my energy for a slide down the hill to the beach. There I studied acupuncture and diet books in search of the cure that seemed to elude me.

Lupus doctors had warned me that exposure to the sun was harmful, but I discarded this advice. Every summer since I was a small child I had been in the sun with no ill effect. I had never shown an adverse reaction. Avoiding the sun denied what I felt was natural and right. Terrified of a reaction, my mother seemed to develop sun sensitivity after she found it could be harmful. She had also experienced that butterfly rash across her cheeks, a condition that I never developed.

I spent one thousand dollars for acupuncture treatments that resulted in a steadily worsening situation. The acupuncturists must have been unscrupulous or oblivious. I wondered if they observed my yellowish caste and my sluggish trip up the single flight of stairs to their center. If so, they might have suggested a trip to the hospital rather than taking money for their procedures. One day they suggested an exercise that involved falling on my back to the ground. It was painful and demeaning. I began to suspect they were taking advantage of me.

Again I ran out of fruit, and I set out for the health food store. Those few blocks seemed like miles. I caught my breath at every other step. Completing the journey was a torturing struggle of will. It was obvious that my diet purification techniques were not working.

Day melted into discouraging day as I slipped into further decline. I lay in my gloomy hotel room, helplessly aware of my life force as it drained away. The specter of death was coming closer.

After two weeks in the motel, I roused myself to fly to Los Angeles and from there to New York. I was to rendezvous with my estranged husband at our farm near Syracuse. On the transcontinental flight my legs and ankles began to swell. After staying overnight with a friend in New York, I arrived the next morning at the Port Authority Bus Terminal with my luggage. The ticket counter was yards away, yet it seemed like miles. I staggered up the steps to the bus.

"Please, sir," I begged the bus driver. "I cannot make it to the ticket counter. Is there another way to purchase the ticket?"

The driver peered down at me. "Sure," he said kindly. "At the first stop in New Jersey."

"Oh, thank you!" I said breathlessly, feeling frail and lonely as I found my seat.

Mercifully, I made it to Syracuse. David met me and we drove to the farm. That night we made love. He was so responsive, so passionate. It was as if we had never been apart. I felt taken care of, appreciated. Swept up in the moment, we were together again. Our lovemaking was a memorial to the love we had shared. It had been a great love. David had written me love poems. He had nurtured my creativity through his example. He had given me so much. On this night, I loved him as much as the day we had met.

I savored the moment. We were back at the farm, our special retreat. I loved the farm with its special memories of our life together. I reveled in the exquisite antiques throughout our rough-hewn bedroom, the special bunk beds made by local craftsmen for guests. There were no televisions, no radios—only our breathtaking view of the mountains.

After this warm reception, I held out the hope that we could reconcile. Unfortunately, David was not a willing caretaker. Maybe it was my fault. After all, I had seemed to know what I was doing when I married him. Consciously, I had set up the relationship to facilitate his daily round, not to make his life more difficult. This was not what he had expected. Now, when I needed his support the most, he refused it. The renewed intimacy was a cruel tease.

The next morning David left me in the emergency room. I felt small and powerless as I was placed on a cold table. There was no fighting spirit left in me. I could take my leave now. I had earned it. I released my hold on life and allowed the weakness to wash over me. Gently, like a glistening tide, my life force ebbed away.

Suddenly, I found myself in another dimension. A glowing golden tunnel appeared in front of me. Far, far into the tunnel, almost as if at its distant opening, stood a man dressed in a splendid golden robe. A luminous white light emanated from behind his magnificent form. With a small smile on his barely intelligible features, he beckoned to me gently. There was a transcendent peace about him, yet I sensed incredible power. The Master continued his invitation, but he was so far away. I strained to make out the features of his face. I wanted to fly to him. I knew that this was possible; it was simply a matter of making the decision. I felt curiosity but no fear. Exiting my body would be an easy choice. I would float through this glorious tunnel and seek the answers the Master had to offer.

Yet, just as I slipped into the tunnel something pulled me back. While I was surrendering to the marvelous force that had come to claim me, the hospital staff had worked to pull me out of my coma with massive doses of cortisone. I remember nothing after the tunnel experience until three days later.

On the third morning, I awakened to a new life. Outside my window was a giant blue spruce that almost obscured the majestic mountains behind it. I put my hands together in thanks, realizing that the earth was again my home. I had survived my near-death experience. I now had a profound initiation into the nature of what lies beyond. Knowing that I would live, I opened my heart to grace. My egocentric will had been unsuccessful in curing the imbalance that had caused my flare; that message was clear.

My rejection of cortisone therapy had led me on a fascinating journey of alternative cures. Unfortunately, my search occurred while in a state of crisis. The gentler preventive measures I investigated would work, but only to prevent a flare. Once I had a flare I must rely upon cortisone—this was a fact that I had refused to accept. I almost gave my life to prove that I could survive without cortisone. Now, again, cortisone therapy had saved me. My fighting will surrendered in light of this admission. Grudgingly I accepted the fact that lupus had become real within me. I abhorred the treatment, but saving me to life on this exquisite planet was preferable to dying too soon. Now, increasingly, this became a joyful return, full of the shining promise of life.

My odyssey had taken me across the country to the mountains of Aspen and the sunny shores of San Diego to seek solutions for the loss of health that separated me from others. Yet throughout this slow decline, a path opened into the spirit world. Without a strong physical tie binding me to earth, I floated closer toward that other realm. The afterlife was perfection, grace and joy—a peace that surpasses anything on earth. As my vitality was slowly renewed, I realized that while the issues I had come here to address were not resolved. I would now realize—and accept—when treatments were undeniably necessary.

The doctors of Cooperstown became interested in my hemolytic anemia manifestation. There were few cases of lupus in this small hospital. The staff was young and curious, and hemolytic anemia was somewhat rare. They were interested in my T-cells, the indicators of an immune system gone awry. Because I might give them more information about my condition, and because they were a progressive group of doctors, I attended meetings in which I was the topic of discussion. Again, there was the possibility of removing my spleen. Fortunately, the cortisone therapy reversed the hemolytic process. My positive response to the therapy again enabled me to escape with my spleen intact.

Soon, however, the harrowing aspects of prednisone therapy burst upon my awareness. (Prednisone is a derivative of cortisone. Prednisone and cortisone can be interchanged.) My moods catapulted from frustration to jubilation. "Better this than a low level indifference!" I wrote in my journal, hearkening back to my dark days in the hotel at Pacific Beach. It became necessary to sift through the adrenal stimulation to determine what my real emotions were. Sleep was difficult and meditation impossible.

There were also physical changes. As a woman in her late twenties, I regarded my appearance as important. After some time on cortisone, I had developed a moon face. The round-cheeked person who looked back at me in the mirror was not one I recognized. My appetite increased, my stomach ballooned. I gained weight in my upper arms. Though I was thin during my recent hemolytic manifestation, people often commented that I looked well. Nevertheless, my body was useless without vital red blood cells. Now, appearance notwithstanding, new life surged through me and I had recovered the will to live. All this was made possible by cortisone therapy. I could accept this tradeoff for another chance at life.

VII.

Alone

The hospital was virtually empty. Therefore, as a favor, my violin was brought to my room. I picked it up, marveling at our reunion after my bridge to death. I chose to begin with the profound melodies of the *Bach Chaconne*. I had performed this piece in the concert hall down the hill from our farm. The chords floated through the corridors of the hospital, resounding from my spacious room overlooking the beautiful Adirondack Mountains. The Cooperstown Hospital had brought me back to life, but the rebirth had come at a price. My marriage was over. It was time to go home, alone. Friends of my husband's picked me up at the hospital. It felt strange to be with them as a single person. David had admired these people. They were mavericks. Fred had been a conscientious objector in World War I. Their elegant white one-story home was perched on the crest of a hill overlooking their gardens and fields. They planted their own food and preserved their crops. Now, without the secure expectations inherent in my role as David's wife, they found our relationship awkward. Not given to small talk, they were completely at a loss how to approach me. With little ceremony, they deposited me in our barn.

Though it was good to be free from hospital intrusions, the silence was deafening as I sat in David's favorite chair. I allowed myself to cry for what might have been. The golden afternoon light sifted through the windows and illuminated my favorite things in this once romantic space. Envisioning beautiful possibilities in the rough-hewn boards, I had made it my project, dragging David to Bloomingdale's to help me pick out rugs and futons. I was proud of the result. The barn seemed so empty without him. I savored the memories, recalling my weaving lessons, our forages into the nearby town's bowling alley for pastrami sandwiches, and our runs in early autumn that crossed the crystal-clear mountain stream near our home. The air was so pure I wanted to bottle it. I drew it deep down into my lungs, trying to save a reserve for my return to the clogged city.

Dan and his wife Terry were our neighbors. However, unlike Fred and his wife, they had lived here all their lives. Dan could fix anything. David, given to poetic license, called him the mountain man. We passed their house on our early evening runs. They invariably invited us into their crowded kitchen, where we sat around the table that held the newest litter of flea-infested kittens. Dan and Terry loved animals. Though they lived their lives on the edge of poverty, Dan was proud of his freedom. Life was hard for them. Dan did tree work when he could find it and some janitorial jobs in the barn down the hill where I had performed the *Chacconne*. I would miss them. Leaving here was too sad to face, but I had no choice.

Fresh mint proliferated in our backyard. Another of my projects had been to hire a backhoe to level the steep hill behind the barn. Since I had converted it from the burdock-infested mess it had been, it was *my* backyard. David and I always took our morning coffee on the patio overlooking the stream. Today I sat on the patio alone listening to the wind in the trees and the occasional screech of a hawk. This would be my last communion with our retreat.

I summoned the memory of the day that David had devastated me. We had donned flannel shirts and corduroy jeans for the long walk to the cliffs on the upper properties. It was a damp, chilly afternoon. The heavy mist settled into my bones, but the silence between us was even more ponderous with unspoken emotions. After about a half an hour we arrived at an abandoned mill covered with lichens and moss. The ominous undercurrent propelled us forward as we plunged deeper into the forest, imagining creatures of the darkness emerging from every shadow.

Miles passed before David turned and spoke. He wore a hard expression I had not seen before.

"Marilyn, I have something to say."

"Yes?"

"I don't love you." A flame of fear seared my stomach.

"But we can work it out, David. I love you."

"That may be true, but I don't love you and haven't for some time. That's all."

"Isn't there a chance we could..."

"There is no chance for anything. I want a divorce. It's over, Marilyn." I started to cry. David turned and walked away with an intractable, intractable look on his face.

Almost six months had passed since that day when I knew that we would never share the farm again. After bringing myself to death and back I had proven that I would survive. Squaring my shoulders, I packed my bags and left. I returned to the city and moved into a studio apartment alone. Though my self-esteem had plummeted, though I allowed myself to feel rage for the first time since my health crisis and channeled my raw emotions into the violin. It was a big step to forge a life alone, and particularly difficult in my weakened condition, but the time had come to face myself in earnest.

My violin was my companion again. I admired my long-lost friend. It was like a beautiful lover. I knew every inch of its dark brown varnish and sensual curves as well as I knew my own body. The sides reminded me of an Italian painting, or an ancient map, with snaking lines of age pointing to random destinations. The back was made of one piece of wood with a flame that flashed yellow highlights when pivoted in the light. I had bought the violin when I was a junior in college. After my parents gave us a price range, Dr. Topper had sent away for instruments for me to try. When I first picked up this violin and played its open strings, it was almost as if the violin was singing me a siren song and drawing me to its lair. My beautiful violin was a living entity, the bearer of my dreams; the focus of my striving to become the best violinist I could be.

Shortly after returning to the city, I gave a recital and played the *Chaconne*. Less than two weeks later, through a tape made from this recital, I won a scholarship to the Nathan Milstein Master Class in Zurich, Switzerland. Nathan Milstein was one of the world's greatest violinists. This was a glorious confirmation that I was moving in the right direction.

My illness and near-death experience had been the impetus for this reclamation. During the months I was too sick to play, I sought the company of my colleagues. At the Aspen Music Festival, I had longed to be a part of the great music I heard. My lack of health set me apart, but it also gave me a viewpoint those performers would never know. What a privilege it is to play great music.

Owning a precious instrument was an awesome responsibility. I often contemplated the other artists who had brought it to life. Many violinists had played on it in the ten generations that came before me. Constant, vigilant commitment was required for me to realize the difficult task of mastery. Some days it was a capricious lover: others, a four-stringed monster, when, at best, it all seemed an uphill battle.

Slowly, uncertainly, my life was opening up, though I was still reeling from a sense of inadequacy fostered by my failed marriage. For some time after my move back to Manhattan, I nursed the hope that we would be together again. However, one bleak day David informed me on the telephone that there would never be reconciliation. At first, I allowed myself to grieve. The devastation I felt mitigated any other response. However, in dying to the possibility of hope, I noticed signs that emotional scars were healing.

I finally loosened the shackles of false dreams, working through my anger. For the first time in my life, I nurtured myself. It was not easy. I contemplated giving up and leaving New York. Emotions overwhelmed me, leaving me broken and useless. I searched deep inside for something, a shred of strength, to anchor my tiny, tossed ship.

I burrowed in my apartment like a wounded animal. My negative self-esteem continually blocked me. Certain that no one would find me attractive or interesting, I became a hermit. Yet it was David himself who had encouraged my creativity. Following his past urgings, my self-expression spilled into other mediums. I created pieces of fiber art. I filled volumes with poetry.

My encounter with death had put life in perspective, and the priorities of my own life were again emerging. I would study the great music that attracted me to the violin. I vowed to realize my dream of performing works I particularly loved. The dark, brooding, harmonies of the Sibelius Concerto had always reminded me of Iceland. After months of preparation, I performed the piece with an amateur orchestra on Long Island. It was a great accomplishment to step in front of the orchestra as a soloist, a dream realized.

After I returned to my apartment there was a telephone message engaging me to perform as a soloist in a double concerto called *Tabula Rasa* in Alice Tully Hall at Lincoln Center. The Armenian composer Arvo Part wrote it. With only two weeks to prepare, I worked without stopping, grateful to have this opportunity. The rehearsals went well. However, the night before the concert I had second thoughts. I called my mother.

"I can't do it!" I told her.

"Can't do what?"

"Stand up in front of God and the New York critics and play a concerto!"

"Yes, you can, Marilyn. You are prepared, you are talented and you deserve this. I am so proud of you! I remember driving you across town to your violin lessons with Mr. Fougerousse in Terre Haute. Now look how far you have come! You can do it. Just stand up there and play. Courage!"

Boosted by my Mother's encouragement, I faced the music. *Tabula Rasa* was written in the violinistic key of A minor. It was reminiscent of Vivaldi—with modern flourishes, one in which a prepared piano creates a sound like an explosion in the middle of the piece. Arvo Part was a mystic. His music's spiritual quality was satisfying, though personally he bore a startling resemblance to David. The second solo violinist, Jeffery Michaels, was a first-rate player. I was to lead the orchestra as concertmaster for the rest of the program. Before the concerto, I went offstage and changed into the white gown I had worn for the Sibelius. In spite of my terror, we garnered a fine review.

The completion of this concert marked a change in my life. I had realized several important goals, but I did not feel complete living alone. I enjoyed the challenge of making it on my own in the city. I had learned a lot about myself; but there were lonely nights of insomnia. I did not feel whole without a real relationship. I was over thirty and determined not to let more time pass before I acted. One night, feeling particularly lonely, I assessed my male friends for possibilities. Who was handsome, intelligent and available?

Tim Malosh had been a friend for years. We had toured together in The Erick Hawkins Dance Company. One night, while on tour at Duke University in North Carolina, we found a bar and partied with the dancers. Tim danced with his girlfriend, the lead dancer. I watched, intrigued, as his slate-gray shoes shuffled across the floor with slick accuracy. Tim had a reputation as a great flutist. Erick, the former husband of Martha Graham, had created a piece for Tim and the company called *Greek Dreams*. At our most recent Opera Orchestra of New York rehearsal, he had offered his umbrella on a rainy day. What a gentleman! I thought, smiling. "It's worth a try," I said to myself as I dialed his number.

Tim was not home. I left a message on his machine and waited two weeks for a reply. During that time, I learned that his father had died. He had just returned from the funeral in Michigan. It was a pivotal event in Tim's life. His father was a complicated man; loving, but very judgmental.

On our first date, we shared a romantic meal of Thai food where everything seemed perfect. Tim was funny and complex. After that first night, we were inseparable. We fell in love and six months later were married.

I had found my life's mate. Tim and I formed a polarity. We were opposites. Tim was a rooted individual. His pragmatic nature was foreign to me, but it would bring me closer to the world I had wanted to leave. Sadly, flare-ups of lupus would soon shatter this new security. From the beginning of our marriage, I would confront this strange disease in ways I would not have believed possible.

VIII.

Pneumonia

In the third month of my marriage, I developed a flare. Again, during the formation period, I ignored the symptoms – fatigue, anemia, weight loss and a low-grade fever. I was teaching at the University and performing concerts. In addition, I decided to prepare an orchestra audition that added extra hours of practice and uncertainty over the outcome. In my rush to achieve success as well as maintain the thin body image expected of young women today, I paid little attention to my eating habits and subsequently became anemic. The doctors at Cooperstown had recommended my new physician. Unfortunately, Dr. Charles Christian also prescribed the hated cortisone in an attempt to reverse the disease process.

In spite of my compromised health, we decided to visit Tim's relatives in Detroit for our first Christmas together. The Maloshes accepted me completely. Tim's mother Jacklyn gave me the love she bestowed upon all of her children. We attended a Christmas Eve ceremony at her mammoth church in the heart of downtown Detroit, enjoying the sound of their magnificent organ enhanced by the acoustics of the church.

We stayed with Melissa, Tim's younger sister, her husband John and their son Benjamin. Melissa had encountered many health problems as a child and Tim had been her protector. Unfortunately, Tim would soon become my protector as well. Benjamin, Melissa's son, was an exceptional child who had inherited his mother's afflictions. In the process of battling them he had developed an inner strength which set him apart. His verbal articulation was also far beyond that of a typical three-year-old. I was delighted when he repeated melodies I played on the piano in an ingenuous soprano with perfect pitch.

That evening, after Melissa and I had checked that Benjamin was asleep, I retired to their renovated attic. Tim and John remained downstairs celebrating Christmas. As soon as I went to bed, my head began to swell. Sleepless minutes grew into hours as my nasal passages, throat and lungs became blocked. Each breath became a terrifying struggle. Around two a.m. Tim came upstairs and immediately went to sleep. I tried to awaken him but he responded with loud, rhythmic snores, his body like stone. My head grew larger and larger. My throat was blocked; my breaths came in shallow gasps. I held on, listening to the loud ticking of the clock. If I could make it to dawn, I might survive. After four more sleepless hours during which my head continued to swell, dawn arrived. At six o'clock, when I woke Tim, my head looked like a pumpkin.

Fortunately, Melissa's best friend was a doctor at a hospital across town. She made a call to get me admitted. Tim brought the car around for our trip to the hospital, twenty miles away. Gasping for breath, my eyes almost swollen shut, I struggled over the icy walkway to the car. Throughout the treacherous ride I huddled in the back seat and struggled to pull air through my blocked throat.

In one swift night, I faced death again. My hemoglobin level registered around four. (A normal level is forty.) A transfusion was necessary to save my life. I received the attention of many doctors that night, but one that stands out was an ear-nose-throat specialist. He burst into my room and, after a perfunctory greeting stuck a tongue depressor down my swollen throat. I could barely open my mouth. Unable to keep this foreign object in my throat without coming up for air, I gagged.

"You're a bad patient!" he said, shaking his finger at me. I was aghast. He was scolding me as I struggled for my life! So I was a bad patient? I was not aware that there were rules for complacent behavior in this situation. What right had he to chastise me? I was furious.

After many hours at my side, Tim returned to Melissa's house. However, in the interim the doctors informed me that there was very little left to do for me. The balance between the hemolytic anemia therapy of high doses of steroids and the intravenous antibiotic for the pneumonia was a delicate one. They discussed the removal of my spleen, but my condition was too fragile. I called Tim.

"Tim, I hate to tell you this, but the doctors say I might not make it. If you don't come back tonight you may never see me alive again."

"I'll be there as soon as I can," he said grimly. Tim bundled up, got back in the car and negotiated the icy roadways to the hospital. The battle for my life raged on as I slipped in and out of consciousness. My soul hovered between control and the beckoning ease of surrender to a higher, more beneficent force. However, even as I prepared to exit my body I felt my husband's energy pulling me down, tugging my soul back to the struggle, urging me to choose life. I continued to vacillate between dimensions, but on this occasion, the bodily struggle seemed closer to my awareness. I could not cross into that peaceful beckoning I yearned to follow. As I faded in and out of consciousness, my spirit longed to break free of this death grip and just to leave it all. Yet I fought on, aided by Tim's amazing psychic power. He did not want to lose me so soon after we had found one another.

After three hours, Tim called my father.

"Marilyn is very ill, Dad."

"My God. What is it? Lupus?"

"Not really, though the flare was a factor."

"I'll be right there."

"I'm taking care of it. She's stabilized now."

"Don't worry. I am coming. I'll get Louise to take care of Ione."

Dad drove from Virginia to Detroit in a single day. I would always be his little girl who needed Daddy to make things all right. Meanwhile, Mother was fading. My father had taken an early retirement fearing that their time together would be short. They had designed a beautiful house with skylights and a single floor to accommodate Mother's difficulty with steps. It was just across the field from Nannie and Louise, overlooking Carter's Creek. Mother would live her final years surrounded by her land, her water and the family she loved.

Unfortunately, just as the house was completed, my mother's health plummeted. She became a subject for research at the National Institute of Health, free of charge. After a three-month hospital stay, she returned home with hideous braces binding her beautiful hands. She had had a difficult time recovering from cataract surgery. For months, she was almost blind and used a magnifying glass to read or create her crafts. Afterwards, she wore glasses with thick lenses. My father had been steadfast in his nursing duties. I sensed that he could use a break and a visit with me provided that, although poor Dad was traveling from one invalid to another. Dad was a hero, and not only as a Marine in World War Two. This healing mandate brought out his sterling qualities. He accepted the task of caring for us both with dignity.

Finally, my crisis passed. During the two weeks of hospital prison, I was required to run the full course of intravenous antibiotics prescribed to cure pneumonia. The weather in Detroit was snowy, the air crisp. My single room overlooked another building where a pebbled pavement covered the rooftop with a large silver fan protruding from its center. In spite of my illness I felt warm and sheltered, enjoying my small portion of blue Northern sky, where the wispy clouds stretched across it like gauze.

The nurses in Detroit were intelligent and compassionate. Though Jacklyn visited every other day, I sensed a reticence. She had nursed George, Tim's father, through a prolonged illness. The wounds must have been fresh. Even so, her kindness made me feel cherished. I admired her quiet dignity, her Christianity in action.

On New Year's Eve, we celebrated in my room. Tim had been the first baby of the New Year in Detroit in 1952. For this double holiday, Tim brought root beer and my father joined us in non-alcoholic cocktails. It was great fun, although I was hooked up to the abominable IV and confined to bed. We celebrated my survival, enjoying our first Christmas season together. I may have been ill, but priceless love was worth more than any gift.

My doctor, Dr. Dilovsky, reminded me of Mickey Mouse. However, he was attentive and efficient. He explained that I had developed pleuritis, an inflammation of the membranes of the lungs and thoracic cavity.

During my hours of solitude, I sifted through the chain of events leading to my incarceration. I was overworked, but that was normal for me. Thus, it was difficult to understand why my body had turned against me. Finally, I decided that I had approached my work in the wrong spirit. I had resented my teaching and I had practiced without joy. Everything had become a chore because I was not connected to the reasons behind my actions. Now that my husband and I were pulling together, I could work toward playing full-time, could indeed work joyfully. This was my dream.

The doctors had saved me from death again. Yet, although my near-death experiences had removed the fear of death, I still was not clear about the direction my life was taking. My high standards often prevented me from relaxing, though, in another sense, I let go completely by allowing my new husband to take care of me. I thought hard about the course of my recent flare. Again, my body had responded with inner warfare. How had this happened? It was possible that I had allowed harmful, habitual thought patterns to take hold during the time I lived alone. Now, because, of thought-patterns that said I was unworthy, on some inner level, I felt the proud necessity to hold myself together. I did not 'need' to manifest a flare. Now that I had a secure base, I could release that necessity. Although I had reached an understanding about why the flare had occurred, I was furious with myself for letting it happen. I seemed to have learned nothing from my hemolytic experience.

At the end of my two-week antibiotic therapy, the doctors released me. I was euphoric over my freedom but it proved to be short-lived. I would return to the hospital sooner than I could have imagined.

IX.

Discoid

I returned to New York, having left the hospital taking 60 milligrams of prednisone each day. I was apprehensive that yet another strange illness would strike without warning. Even so, I was thrilled to be home again. Though weakened from my bout with pneumonia, I puttered around the house and even trimmed an asparagus fern, one of my favorite plants.

The next day, I called Mother. Though she was not a smoker, due to lupus-related cortisone therapy for the lungs, she had developed a case of emphysema. She was usually in bed now. My mother had her own problems, and yet I knew she could empathize with me. But I was also almost afraid to talk to her and commiserate about our conditions. Together we seemed to magnify the situation.

"How are you, Mother?" I asked.

"Dr. Gravatt says I may need a wheelchair, darling."

I recalled Mother's mention of her great-aunt who had languished in a wheelchair with rheumatoid arthritis. Mother told me how she had felt sorry for her, but I sensed that she admired her relative's courage. Now she would become, like her relative, an invalid. Mother continued. "And I might be going back to N. I. H."

"Oh," I muttered. "Don't you miss Dad when you're gone?"

"Of course. However, it gives him a break from caring for me. And there are wonderful crafts there. I've just finished a macrame plant hanger."

"But, Mother, it's a hospital! Don't you wish you could be at home?"

"Sometimes. Yes, often I do," she said softly, pausing for another shallow breath. "Marilyn, I may be helping to find a cure. They are trying new therapies on me. I have to do it, Marl. And how are you? Are you recovering? Are you resting?"

"I've been fine. You know that. I'm perfectly able to handle myself," I asserted. I needed to be strong for me as much as Mother in spite of my weakened state. Yet, as we talked, something in her voice spurred me to an irrational panic. I could not cope with my mother's invalidism. It was too close. I watched in horror as a blister appeared on my forearm. Then one on my leg, then a blister on the other leg—like time-lapse photography! Somehow, our talk had triggered a release within my body that responded with this bizarre result.

I was stunned at this demonstration of the power of thought. It now seemed apparent that while I was taking a large dose of prednisone a host of strange illnesses could become real within me during a compressed period. This drug had the power to destroy me. Prednisone exaggerated all my responses, and the drug aided my subconscious need to suffer. It was, I was to discover, a dermatological manifestation of lupus—another instance which allowed the 'great impersonator' to present me with an opportunity for self-immolation.

When Tim arrived home, he found me in the bedroom.

"What happened to you? Did you burn yourself?"

"No, Tim," I cried. "This just happened."

"What do you mean?"

"These blisters formed this morning!" I exclaimed. "I watched myself create them while I was talking to Mother on the phone!"

"Nonsense. That is impossible. There must be some other explanation. You might have had a reaction to that asparagus fern. We'll call Dr. Christian first thing tomorrow morning."

"Great," I smirked. Tim knew I hated to consult the doctor. Nevertheless, the next day I entered the Hospital for Special Surgery. The doctors were not sure what had caused the reddish-purple lesions now covering most of my body. These lesions appeared on one side of my body one day and on the opposite side a few days later. This mirror effect was a common manifestation of lupus. It was similar to joint pain which 'transferred' to the other side of my body. The doctors presumed it was lupus masquerading as a skin disorder, but as a precaution I was quarantined to a single room to watch my body create new sickle-shaped lesions, each of which was accompanied by stinging pain.

Dr. Christian had recommended a dermatologist. Dr. Bean gave me a hasty examination, seeming repulsed by the sores on my body. He doesn't care about me or my condition, I thought. Obviously wanting to complete our transaction, he prescribed an ointment for each lesion every two hours, twenty-four hours a day. After four days of this miserable therapy the doctor visited again.

"Doctor, I've been applying this ointment every two hours. I cannot sleep. Couldn't you allow me to lessen the frequency?"

"Oh, it's not necessary to apply the ointment continually," he replied offhandedly.

"What?" I shouted. "My condition is worse now because you gave me the wrong instructions! I could not sleep, and that was my only relief. But I'm sure the extent of my suffering is of no concern to you."

The doctor stared at me, incredulous, as if I was a talking robot. My words had no effect. I was furious. I had given my trust to him, and I felt betrayed. Again, I felt the reality of imprisonment. I could not leave my room until the antibiotic course was again completed. One afternoon the hospital pastor visited. He was a slight man with a bad complexion and thinning, sandy hair.

"Hi, Marilyn. I'm Father O'Flanigan," he began, offering his hand and a small card that contained a prayer for the sick. I was in no mood to welcome an unbidden visitor, yet another of the pantheon that paraded through my room at arbitrary intervals throughout the day. "And how is the healing proceeding?" he asked kindly.

"Frankly, Father, it's very discouraging. I have just gotten over pneumonia, and now I have these strange blisters and I am in constant pain. I cannot seem to stay away from the hospital. Every minute in here seems like an eternity."

"You seem to hold a lot of anger," he suggested gently. "Might it be possible for you to let this anger direct the healing phase of your life?" I nodded, intrigued. It was a novel concept, but it made little sense to me. Instead of anger, I wished I could harness the healing power of love that seemed so far from my grasp. Now I could blame myself for another powerless condition.

"Saint Paul said that through his pain God was made greater in him. When he was strong, God was less in him," the Pastor said, looking into my eyes. After he left, I pondered his words. Did this mean that if one was suffering, the strength required greater faith? Did it mean that one could come closer to God through suffering than by any other means? That when one was well they were unable to attain a state of grace? I felt far away from God, far away from loving myself. I was functioning on a survival level, hanging on while in chaos of the unnatural emotions evoked by prednisone. As I gritted my teeth through the pain of open blisters on my body, God seemed less in me, not more.

At times I detached from my suffering and observed the red lesions. The force creating these patterns followed quantifiable rules, or universal laws, which could never be broken. These physical lesions were a direct consequence of my thoughts. Though I believed that the prednisone had speeded up the creation of the lesions, I also recognized that I had somehow initiated them through the force of my intent.

Tim's friend Craig invited him to perform a recital at the University of Louisiana. Craig had been a dancer with the Erick Hawkins Dance Company. Though we were thrilled at the prospect of the extra income,

I was dismayed to discover that the hospital stay had seriously depleted my physical strength.

"It's only ten days, Marilyn," Tim said as he held my hand. "And you know how much we need the money. I just can't pass it up."

"Of course," I replied. "Besides, you need to get away and spend some time with Craig. It must be lovely down there. Do not worry about me. I'll be fine." I smiled, hoping to look convincing. The days passed as I fought to remain calm through the mood swings caused by the large dose of prednisone.

Finally, the waiting was over. Tim would be arriving home soon. He called me. I was thrilled to hear his voice.

"How was Louisiana?" I asked, hoping to hear a pleasant account of balmy evenings. Instead, Tim's voice was tense.

"We're broke, Marilyn. I am staving off the creditors. So many doctor bills! Our insurance covers such a small percentage. And you know how much extra income I gave up to stay with you in Detroit." Tim replied. "I think I alienated Craig with my constant worry over your condition. However, there is some good news. I've spoken to Dr. Christian."

"What did he say?" I asked.

"He is going to release you, but only under the condition that I follow his instructions carefully."

"Oh, Tim! Finally! I can't wait to get out of here."

"Hold on. Only one more day."

I left the hospital, following-up at Dr. Bean's office. It was a spacious wood-paneled space on the Upper East Side. During my hospital stay, I had urged Dr. Christian to bring the prednisone down to a tolerable amount. Accordingly, we had slowly tapered the dosage down to 35 milligrams daily. This was a little easier. A dosage of 20 milligrams or more brought mood swings, insomnia, and severe appearance change. The feeling that I had taken amphetamines increased with each added milligram. A dosage of 60 milligrams was almost unbearable. It was because of these intolerable mood swings that I had urged my doctors to bring me down from the drug as soon as possible. The tapering occurred gradually, 5 milligrams at a time.

Upon entering Dr. Bean's office, I went to an examination room. A nurse's aide directed me to lie down on the table for biopsies. These biopsies taken on the palm of my hand and my right thigh were unnecessary. We never discovered the cause of my condition, even after the results of the biopsies came in.

Afterwards, Dr. Bean whisked into the room. Hesitatingly, I asked, "Doctor, do you think we can arrest this skin problem?"

"Yes," he declared, "even if it takes a dosage of 60, 75 or 80 milligrams!"

I was seething. I had been struggling with high cortisone dosages since November. Now it was late February. I believed that the high steroid dose was responsible for my explosive contraction of pneumonia, and, probably, for the quick manifestation of lupus skin disease. If I were to raise the dosage to his lowest recommendation I would be back to the hideous 'moon-face', the tremendous highs and incredible lows. Just as I was slowly, painstakingly, tapering the steroids down, this doctor had suggested a return trip.

The second hospitalization had weakened me still further, yet I stubbornly refused to accept limitations. I wanted to return to normal life as soon as possible. At night, to lessen the pain of the healing lesions, Tim wrapped my entire body, mummy-like, in wet gauze soaked in saline solution.

His role of caretaker was taking a toll. Though he spent every waking moment waiting on me, Tim felt ineffectual. He became a chain-smoker while I, frustrated at the slow pace of recovery, was ashamed of my appearance. We were alone in the world, holding each other tight, our bond forged through adversity. I was incomplete when Tim was not physically near. This strengthening bond increased the distance between our healthy colleagues and us. They had no frame of reference for what we were experiencing.

I was involved in a new-music group called Musical Elements. We renamed it the Musical Elephants. The scores we performed at Cooper Union were difficult new works that involved mixed forces, usually a violin, viola, cello, trumpet, oboe, clarinet, harp, and trombone. I was self-conscious about my new moon-face appearance but I wanted to get back to work, so I agreed to perform.

I had been the violinist of this group for several years. On the day of our first rehearsal, our cat Max died. He was 15. Max had stayed with me through each illness with loving, healing energy. I sadly made my way to the oboist Vicki's apartment to rehearse. The rehearsal had just begun when I realized that I could not control my bow as I drew it across the strings. I sounded like a beginner. I had accepted this concert while still in the hospital. I was excited at the prospect of a challenging chamber music concert, but in my enthusiasm I had not allowed for recovery time before these more difficult solo performances where I was 'exposed', meaning that every note could be heard. After our first rehearsal, I received a call from the director.

"Marilyn, this is Dan."

"Oh, Hi, Dan," I chirped, my heart fluttering. A call from the conductor was irregular.

"It's probably nothing, but I noticed that you had a little trouble with your part today. I'm sure you can clear it up by the concert."

"Of course, Dan. I am sorry. I'll work on it."

"Thanks, Marilyn."

The month of hospitalization and subsequent physical weakness had affected my playing. I simply was not up to my usual standards. Not only did the long respite from the violin leave me out of shape, but I had also refused to acknowledge the limitations imposed by extreme illness. I wanted so much to return to playing that I had glossed over the severity of my condition. I had not given myself enough time to recuperate. The optimism that had brought me through life-threatening crises was misplaced in this context.

Embarrassed at my lack of control, I got in the practice room and worked hard until the concert—where I played a fine performance. Even so, the concert was a terrifying experience that proved I had returned to performing too soon. My willful nature wanted to rewrite the book of my life the way I would have liked it to be. After the concert, I needed a break. I decided to visit my mother and father in Virginia.

I was still opposed to cortisone treatment. I wanted to get off the drug as soon as I could, but this time I would do it with a doctor's guidance. In the months before I tapered the dose to zero, the side effects of long-term use began to plague me. I lost hair and developed a chubby face and spindly legs. I sported a round, pregnant-looking stomach. I cut my hair very short to make my hair loss less obvious. However, the other symptoms remained.

It was hurtful to see my mother when a new complication greeted me with each visit. Nannie treated her like a delicate princess, begging her to rest after the slightest exertion. This had been Nannie's response for many years. It was her way of preventing health problems for her daughter. Yet, she also deliberated over each new ache and pain. It was her attempt to control a powerless situation, but it was too much, almost an obsession. And in spite of everyone's efforts, Ione continued to decline.

Mother must have known, when she planned the house next to her mother and sister, that this place would see her fade away just as it had birthed and raised her. Though her music and her family had taken her far away, there had been no doubt that she would return. Here in her regal bedroom, Louise and Nannie cherished every moment with her. There was always laughter; no matter what condition Mother was battling. This room became the hub of our gatherings. She had designed it with a subtle floral pattern and a flaming red carpet. The blinds matched the carpet and wallpaper—red on one side and white on the other. Mother was a Leo. Although she might not have thought of it consciously, the reds, like the flame of her fire sign, probably energized her and aided in healing.

Though I enjoyed the support of my closest relations I also felt impotent. It was comforting to be a link in an unbroken line between my grandmother, Mother and myself. We visited, exchanged stories in the Southern way and simply enjoyed being together, even as we concealed our sadness at Mother's limitations.

From the time I was a toddler, when Mother's gorgeous dresses adorned us and Dad dutifully chronicled them in photographs, Mother and I loved being pretty. However, as an adult with a disease that destroyed my appearance, I could not cope with the expectations of my relatives. There is a tacit Southern belief that appearance is more important than substance. The disease had certainly altered Mother's appearance. After the cataract operation, she wore bottle-thick glasses. Her hands were contorted by rheumatoid arthritis. Moreover, every breath was becoming a struggle and she could not eat. Mother reveled in her thinness and bought beautiful outfits to adorn the figure she had finally achieved. Though she made the best of her bodily changes, when it became obvious that she could never have a normal look, she transferred many of her expectations to me. I could feel her disappointment as her own loss of control was mirrored in my situation. This left me frustrated, feeling set apart and a disappointment to those around me.

The disparate nature of my appearance only served to illuminate my inner conflicts. I could not bear to look in the mirror and see a stranger. The more I tried to control this disease the more it seemed to spin out of control. Prednisone had saved my life, but at what cost? I envisioned a future spotted with episodes of prednisone-induced depression. This ever-weakening condition stared at me as my mother. She was an invalid with concerned relatives to protect her, but a restricted invalid nonetheless.

No, I was not ready for long-term cortisone therapy. Yet, running away was not the solution. I had proven that. It seemed to me that my mother's unquestioning acceptance of, even reverence for, medical solutions was partially responsible for her dilemma.

Because our bond was strong, I wanted desperately to give my mother the cure which seemed beyond her grasp—for her sake as well as my own. I still believed that by unearthing the unseen causes of 'my' disease I might discover the direct relationship between buildup and manifestation. During my *satori* revelation, I saw my hand moving through space and creating the thinnest of webs. This showed me that each materialization had a cause. If I could learn what made blisters appear on my hands, my head swell up like a pumpkin, or my mother's hands draw up into gnarled knots, I might begin to reverse it. I left Virginia resolved to find the answer.

X.

A Man Who Heals

During the summer of 1985, I stumbled upon the work of Edgar Cayce while seeking an alternative lupus cure. Cayce gave psychic readings through the 1940's and advised a few people with lupus. I ordered copies of his readings and eagerly combed them for clues that would set me free. Though the readings were not as helpful as I would have wished, I was inspired to join the Association for Research and Enlightenment. This became a beneficial alliance for me.

The A.R.E. Press publishes metaphysical books that enlarge upon many of the concepts I was discovering. I learned about auras. In addition, I found that certain colors could heal or stimulate. Cayce described the seven chakras, or energy centers, which were vortices of swirling energy located at certain points near the body. East Indian yogis had been aware of chakras for thousands of years. During my enrollment at the Manhattan School, I had used chakras in my yoga practice. While concentrating on my 'third eye', I brought my energy up from the base of my spine and through the top of my head. This procedure enabled me to awaken my psychic abilities. Now I returned to this practice, sending energy to correct imbalances located through illness.

I already knew of the healing power of music, but from Cayce I learned that great music exists in a realm of higher vibration. Here is where our immortal soul, or higher self, dwells. A sojourn in this dimension can free us from the lower emotions and create an elevation that is necessary for healing. Music facilitates arrival very quickly by speaking directly to our souls. As a professional performer, I had tapped into this force for many years. Playing or listening to works of the great masters allows access to a vast current of energy.

I ordered courses on metaphysical subjects through the A. R.E. In a past lives course I found that certain foods, styles of architecture and cultures felt familiar while others brought a certain aversion. I loved the Japanese culture. My familiarity with Zen Buddhism had defied logical explanation. How could I, a Western woman, somehow 'know' the experience of *satori* when I had never studied Buddhism formally? In an experience known as self-regression, I discovered that I had indeed been a Japanese man in another lifetime. In this vision, I found myself in a large room. Dressed in a dark blue-and-white robe, I sat at a table and enjoyed the company of friends. I felt happy and comfortable as this man.

Another such regression brought images of a former life as a silversmith in Colonial America. I lived in a primitive forested settlement and worked as a silversmith. I wore a flowing white shirt, knickers and tights, my flowing blonde hair loosely fastened with a ribbon. As I sat hunched over a wooden desk working on a pewter spoon, the late afternoon sun illuminated the worn floorboards of my cottage. These two vivid experiences gave me a personal confirmation of reincarnation.

An even more startling demonstration of reincarnation had occurred several years earlier. Two years before my marriage to Tim I joined a string trio. We named ourselves The Brighton Trio. A Japanese pianist named Masanabu hired us to come to Arcady, Maine. The brilliant cellist, Mike Finckel, was also a composer. We were to perform a Beethoven Trio, a Brahms Piano Quartet and a piece that Mike wrote in Bangor, Maine. Mike borrowed a car and we drove to Boston, where friends made their vacant home available to us. Their mansion, situated high atop a hill, was a spacious Tudor dwelling. The piano room could have been a setting for a Victorian novel. As Mike labored through the night to complete his composition, Monica, the violist in the group, and I roamed the house like children on a treasure hunt. We found several records of early music on which Monica had performed. The next morning we set out for Bangor. We stayed with a family who hosted musicians with the Arcady Festival. Their gray house, standing alone in an empty field, reminded me of a Norman Rockwell painting. Mounds of snow, the crisp northern sky, and the different cast to the light completed the picture.

The night of our arrival they hosted a meeting. One of their members, Alora, was a gifted psychic. After the meeting, she joined the visiting musicians sitting at a long table in their spacious kitchen. Alora was short and rounded, with a few teeth missing. Her hair was a nondescript brown color and her speech was coarse, but there was something about her eyes that magnetized us. She saw straight into our souls.

Alora turned her piercing gaze to Monica, grasping her hand. "All right, Love," she began, pausing to let the messages come. "I see you as a court musician in England. You are playing for the Royal Family." I could imagine Monica in a velvet gown; her bodice strung with pearls and her flowing hair worn in a braid. After our previous night in Boston and Monica's interest in early music, this observation seemed plausible.

Next, she turned to me. Holding my hand and looking into my eyes, she waited again for impressions. "You, Sweetheart, were a harpsichord player." I nodded. When I hear harpsichord music, it 'feels' familiar. I 'remember' the sensation of playing in my hands and the timbre resonates from somewhere deep within me. It was even possible that I might have known Monica as a court musician. My proficiency on the organ, which became my Mother's instrument, matched the feeling of playing the harpsichord.

"And...a dancer...in Paris," she continued. "You rebelled against the structured life. This compromised your career. You could have been a prima ballerina, but you wouldn't allow yourself to release your ego and trust, my dear." Again, a small voice inside knew it was true. I had studied ballet as a child. I had long legs and a short torso—a dancer's body. I remembered the first day that I donned running shoes. Jogging felt like soaring through the air in the ballet improvisations I had enjoyed as a child. I also 'knew' the sensation of flying through the air in time to the music as I performed in the pit with the American Ballet Theater Orchestra.

Alora smiled. "What?" I asked, afraid that she would reveal something too personal. "You were a merchant's daughter in ancient Greece..." She laughed mischievously. "With many male suitors." I laughed, too. "Soon, my love, you will meet a sandy-haired man and the two of you will fall in love and marry. Then you will travel around the world!" she said. I was thrilled. I loved to travel. Though I usually dated men with dark hair, I was to meet Tim, who fit her description perfectly.

I knew with inner certainty that each past life was correct. The factors leading me to agree with her conclusions were not strong physical evidence. Instead, they were inner urgings like the strange familiarity that had brought me to Humphrey's *Concentration and Meditation* and my first *satori* experience. From this impressive display, I decided to learn more about psychics.

After the study of reincarnation, one of the subjects Cayce 'discovered' (at least for Westerners) I began to imagine the possibility of developing Cayce's psychic abilities in people living today. Cayce claimed that we are co-creators with God. If this meant that godlike powers await us, then we must discover how to bring ideas directly into manifest reality. All creations originate as thought. Cayce tuned into these thoughts in his psychic readings. Through the instant appearance of my lesions, I learned that immediate manifestation is indeed possible. Cayce seemed to imply that we could create our lives with more conscious control. This could mean anything from directing our financial futures to curing ourselves of illness. The will, he explained, could direct one's life. However, as I discovered in San Diego, will alone is not enough. It must be an adjunct to the subconscious, or the superconscious—the soul. With these two powers in tandem, the force is like a burgeoning river flowing to the sea.

In the 1940's, reincarnation was not a popular concept in America. Yet Cayce, who was a devout Christian, gave a psychic reading which indicated that he had experienced a past life in Ancient Egypt. He also predicted that he would reincarnate again after his death and lead the masses to greater understanding. This information, given as he was lying on a couch in an altered state of consciousness, was heretical to his Christian faith. Cayce was an introverted, uneducated boy. He was determined, however, to read the Bible throughout once a year. At the age of twelve, an angel visited him. After the visitation, he was able to recite the entire contents of a book left under his pillow the previous night. He could fall into a trance similar to a deep sleep and predict events or dictate natural healing prescriptions culled from reading the 'Akashic records' (a library on the etheric plane where all past, present and future knowledge is stored). His psychic readings, now categorized and studied by people all over the world, emphasized service to others using the example of Jesus Christ. They were not lenient with those who were selfish or greedy.

Edgar Cayce was an exemplary person. At first, he doubted his abilities. But then, after he channeled healing information which saved his son's eye and cured his wife's near-fatal illness, he recognized their reality. He was subsequently careful not to use them for financial gain. He helped those who asked, never turning anyone away. Although he encountered many setbacks, he fought to form a hospital for treatment of people receiving readings. Finally, the Association for Research and Enlightenment was formed at Virginia Beach.

Cayce predicted many events for the new Millennium. Like Nostradamus hundreds of years before, he was able to 'read' the vast negative currents that were the cause and, in turn, effects of wars and natural disasters. It is still too soon to ascertain the accuracy of Cayce's predictions. What does seem obvious, however, is that by taking responsibility for our actions we have a chance to reverse the flow of causation that could spur negative results. Ignoring the laws of nature for temporal personal gain will cause destruction for all. As my *satori* experience showed, we are responsible for each action we generate. One who believes he is above these laws will have to face them whether he is aware of this principle or not.

Scientists have theorized that we use only a small percentage of our brain. There is a vast quantity of psychic information available to us today, and interest in this area is gaining momentum. We are learning to 'co-create with God', as we become stewards of the remaining plant and animal species.

If Cayce's psychic abilities were commonplace, it would reduce the need for courtrooms or hospitals. There is also an etheric plane and a causal or mental plane, where ideas originate before they manifest in dense physical matter. A world where everyone can read the 'Akashic records', or the records of these thoughts, may be far in the future for humans on earth, but I believe this is the direction of our evolution. In a future realization, people would communicate telepathically, they would see into a person's soul on first meeting, and they could master illness and death. They might develop thought systems that would create new vegetation and evolving life forms. Cayce showed us that such amazing skills do await us.

Though I was far from realizing such accomplishments, I did prove that it was possible to control my thoughts. After discovering Cayce, I realized that unknown worlds awaited me. Though I did not consider myself a talented psychic, I had experienced visions that were unexplained.

The year before I married Tim I moved to a one-bedroom apartment on 57th Street where I lived alone and often practiced in front of the living room that featured a mirrored wall. One evening, as I was resting, I gazed into the mirror. Images of myself in past lives paraded before me like a slide show. I saw a wealthy older lady, several Oriental males and an ancient American Indian. At any time after this experience, I could choose to see my features change into that of the old Indian. I was not sure whether he was a guide or a version of me. However, he was always with me any time I changed my focus.

On the recommendation of Cayce's readings, I began a dream journal, searching for clues to lupus. I recorded a recurring dream in which I found myself in the third grade, required to repeat each grade. Mother insisted in the dream that I complete the grades in sequence.

"Marl," she said, "You must finish this grade and then you can go on to the next. In no time, you'll graduate from high school." I nodded, feeling that this was a perfectly logical explanation, although I had already been through high school. Underlying her words, however, was the implication that I had done something terribly wrong. So I dutifully attended school in dream after dream. My sentence seemed interminable. Elementary school was so boring! It was hell, but there was no way out. Unfortunately, I would discover the meaning of this dream soon enough.

Cayce's accomplishments inspired me to put his principles to use. This new technical knowledge had brought another key to self-mastery. I had experienced past lives for myself and had accessed my subconscious through dreams. I hoped that this key would enable me to put lupus behind me. Therefore, I was scarcely prepared for a new attack that almost blinded me in its wake.

Illustrations

Ione George Gibson in 1950, the year before I was born.

Nellie Bly George – Nannie to us. Ione's mother, my grandmother, Circa 1950.

Ione and Louise George in front of Carter's Creek.

The newlyweds - Ione and Robert Gibson in April of 1944.

Ione Gibson performing at the Tides Inn in 1950.

Robert and Ione before children.

The Gibson family in Terre Haute, Indiana in 1963. I am 12, Bob is 10 and Jeff is 8.

Jeff and Bob in Weems, 1974.

Mom and Dad in Spain, 1974.

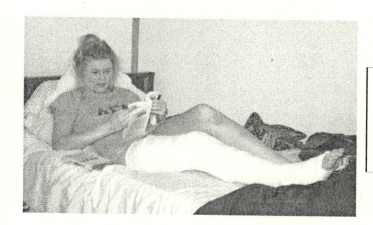

Just after I broke my leg in Iceland, 1974.

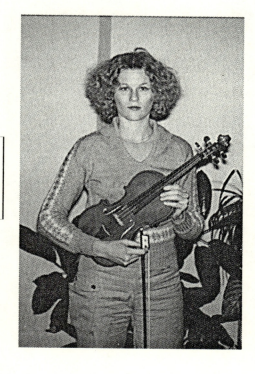

Here I am in 1979 in New York City.

Tim and my wedding day
– September 30, 1984.

Tim and his mother, Jacklyn Malosh – December, 1984.

Tim, me and Dad on Tim's birthday – New Year's Day, 1985, at the hospital in Detroit.

Mom, me and Tim in January of 1986.

Mother at home in March of 1986.

Mother and Dad's last portrait together – 1987.

'Dr. Tim' preparing to insert antibiotic into my peritoneal dialysis catheter.

I was on this CCPD machine for ten hours every night.

My zombie phase — on the peritoneal machine and taking dylantin and phenobarbitol in March of 1989.

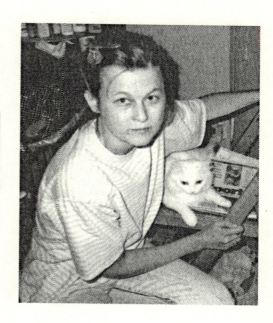

Shortly before the transplant, I had gone back on hemodialysis after an eight-and-a-half month remission.

Bunny with her litter.

After the transplant – Deetsu, me and Diana Smith-Barker.

Tim preparing for *Miss Saigon.*

XI.

Meningitis

It was hot in the summer of 1985 in New York City, and the concrete jungle offered little respite from noise, heat and humidity. After pneumonia in January and the strange blisters in February, this year had not been easy. By June, off the prednisone completely, I spent leisurely afternoons at the Manhattan Plaza Health Club. I lifted weights, took a sauna, and then swam a mile. My swimming meditation of "Love, Peace and Harmony", was repeated with each breath. This purifying process took at least three hours every other day.

One night I attended a party. I had a wonderful time, but I awakened at 7 a.m. the next morning with a splitting headache, nausea, and a temperature of 106. Somehow, Tim realized the necessity for lowering my temperature. He put me in a cold bath to bring it down. Still, my body felt like rubber. By eight a.m., I had lost all sensation in my fingers and arms. At nine a.m. Tim called Dr. Christian, who ordered me to get to the Hospital for Special Surgery immediately. By now, in spite of Tim's efforts, I was hallucinating. He dressed my limp body and carried me through the lobby of our apartment building.

Inside the cab, I vomited, but I was too sick to be embarrassed. The searing headache felt like a knife twisting between my eyes, my body now like a block of cement. Finally, we arrived at the Hospital for Special Surgery. I was put in a wheelchair and rolled upstairs to

Dr. Christian. His face grim, he took my temperature and lifted me back into the wheelchair. Without another word, the doctor wheeled me into the elevator, out the double doors, and across the cobblestone courtyard to the Emergency Room of the New York Hospital.

After I was admitted, the valiant Dr. Christian marshaled the finest specialists in a moment's notice. Viral experts suspected that I had contracted spinal meningitis. After a battery of examinations, I was sent upstairs to the ninth floor. An ice suit controlled my skyrocketing temperature. Again, I was barely in the physical world, preparing to leave my body. Hallucinations crowded my vision as I floated through a pleasant, ethereal dimension. Returning to reality for a check on my body sent me back up into the stratosphere to escape my physical agony.

Hours passed as I slipped in and out of consciousness. When I forced myself to return to my body, the sensation was like tugging fifty balloons down to earth. The force leading me upwards was strong and I was just going with the flow.

As in my previous near-death experiences, it was more difficult to put on the mantle of physicality than to pull it off. None of my hallucinatory images made logical sense, but they did make a tantalizing escape. At the same time, my body continued to develop a fighting will of its own. However, the virus that took me so suddenly was not giving up either. The war raged on until the plastic ice suit and antibiotics took effect. By early morning my temperature had dropped. I returned to lucidity and the pain of recovery.

The onset of meningitis had been amazingly swift, the doctors agreed. I barely escaped death and averted paralysis. Without the swift action of Dr. Christian's staff, I would have spent the rest of my life in a wheelchair. I was lucky to have these superb doctors come to my aid. If I had waited a few hours longer, the scenario would have been completely different.

The disease probably struck swiftly because the two previous hospitalizations had weakened me. If I were taking prednisone, a short viral incubation period would have made more sense. However, I had tapered off my prednisone dosage slowly with Dr. Christian's supervision. He did not speak of it, but I sensed through his resistance that he preferred to have me take a small maintenance dose. I obstinately insisted on being free of the drug. Prednisone can act in strange ways to inhibit the natural immune reflexes of the body. I theorized that this bizarre disease might have been the result of my weakened resistance.

The next day the doctors decided that I needed a spinal tap to ascertain the type of meningitis virus. I was no longer critically ill so they could afford to be cautiously optimistic. My forays into physical fitness had definitely aided the quick turnaround. For the third time, I steeled myself for another two weeks in prison to wait out my intravenous antibiotic program.

Institutional hospital life accommodates employees rather than patients. The doctors examine patients during business hours. This artificial schedule was always a transition for me. My performing schedule was most active in evenings and on weekends, the opposite of most working people's routines. Moreover, during the added stress of sickness, I needed a natural rhythm that would correspond with my healing. When I was tired, I required rest, silence and darkness. When I felt better, I wanted some sustenance and gentle, nurturing companionship. I was so grateful for Tim's visits. Once I began to feel better, I wanted him near me all the time. Unfortunately, visiting hours were limited. The lonely hours stretched each evening after his departure.

The hospital day began with a flurry before and around breakfast, a spurt before lunch, and sporadic visitations until supper. This was the highlight of my day. I savored Tim's visit, holding him close and begging him to stay as long as possible. The excitement subsided after this; there followed a long, lonely time that stretched toward the next morning when the cycle began again. If I was too sick to read, the tiny television sets provided some respite. At night, I struggled to sleep. During these times, monitoring rituals brought a certain comfort. However, the dawn of the long hospital day brought the familiar fishbowl sensation. Being on display in my most disheveled state with a hoard of doctors peering down at me, I felt like the actress in some strange play.

    I had a more intimate relationship with the nurses than the doctors. Nurses on the night shift were talkative. When I could not sleep, I lay in bed eavesdropping on their lives. While my life was in abeyance, I envied these vigorous nurses returning to their husbands and children. My world seemed so far away. During my hospital stay I was offered an opera tour in Italy—I would have loved to go. Leaving my violin was like losing a twin. Therefore, I redefined myself through my position in the hierarchy of the hospital. I could not ascertain if the nurses were sensitive to the difference implied between their active lives and my hibernating one. Obviously, they had entered the profession to help. Though they received less recognition in status and pay than the doctors did, they were often the healers. The more empathetic ones formed bonds that soothed the deepest suffering.

    July ended. Soon I was able to make my way down the hall dragging the IV pole behind me. I was proud to have completed the trip to the patient's lounge, but on my arrival, freakish characters greeted me with blank stares. One, a drug addict, had picked at her IV, her arm inundated with scabs. Other patients were barely coherent.

    My roommate brought her own set of problems. Susan weighed at least three hundred pounds. Her girth confined her to a wheelchair. Unfortunately, my bed faced hers. At night, her labored breathing kept me awake. I marveled that her body could tolerate such a strain. Because I was friendly to her, she decided to fixate upon me.

    We played cards to pass the time and she told me stories about her past. Susan claimed she had been a singer at Juilliard. I was skeptical, so I pressed her for details. She seemed to have little knowledge of the school or even the rudiments of music. I felt sorry for her, but her problems were beyond my scope to fix. Though I attempted to put some distance between us, she had made up her mind that I was her ticket to a normal life.

Susan was skilled at making jewelry and she made me a necklace with several bracelets, charging me a fair price. With the profit from this exchange, she paid her cab fare home. Upon her arrival, she called me at regular intervals. It soon became obvious that she was obsessed with me. Her attention had gone from cloying to stifling. Finally, Tim warned her to back off. After a week, the calls stopped.

My swimming regimen before the hospital stay had brought me to a better state of fitness. Though I began to feel well enough to go home, my two-week antibiotic course was not finished. So I was overjoyed when one sunny afternoon an arts-and-crafts representative brought me a small loom. Ten years earlier I had made a cross-country trip where I found shapely driftwood from the desert. This inspired me to define the form further through adding jute in natural tones. After that beginning, my output had been prolific. My hangings emerged from me almost whole—they always possessed a certain inner logic, as if dictated to me. For some unknown reason they emerged looking distinctly Indian. I wondered if it was a former life as an American Indian, or my Indian guide, which had produced this expression through me.

It was satisfying to have a creative outlet at last. In spite of the omnipresent IV in my arm, I created a weaving in earth tones. Still, as the waiting stretched on, I could not shake the feeling that I should not be here, and that I was missing the joy of making music.

On July 28, I wrote, "I wonder if the rest of my life will be spent in hospitals. The core of my soul is in abeyance here. I do not understand how people can be in this world without music. I feel as if I am separate from everyone else. When can I live again?"

The final week dragged by. Outside my window the blazing summer sun beckoned. In a heartbeat, I would, if I could, be in the 'free world'. It was so near, yet so far away. I had relocated to a large room with four beds where curtains with large violet-and-yellow checks formed partitions for privacy. One afternoon a small brunette woman arrived. She was around 75 and seemed to have Alzheimer's disease. Physically vigorous, she would not stay in bed. One night she picked out her IV and wandered aimlessly through the hall. When the nurses discovered she was free, they strapped her to the bed. The poor woman was helpless, completely at their mercy. She could not reach the call button to request help. My heart ached for her. I summoned the nurses frequently on her behalf but felt unauthorized to challenge their decision. They believed she was a danger to herself. Yet, to me she often seemed lucid and aware of her condition.

How easy it is to become a statistic. A procedure could be irreversible—there is always the possibility of slipping into a coma or of taking the wrong drugs. My instinct for self-preservation surfaced at times like this. I had barely escaped with all my organs intact and had narrowly slipped past paralysis and death. All of my hospital experiences had brought me successfully out of crises, but I was careful to look out for myself. I may have been a nameless patient to some, but I made sure that this was not true for others. I had emerged unscathed partially because of this wary attitude and a hands-on approach regarding my medication. Caring for a patient with happy results is the rule in hospitals, and this is wonderful. I just did not want to be the unhappy exception.

My two weeks finally at an end, I prepared to leave my elderly friend in the bed next to me. For my part, having richly earned my freedom, I anxiously awaited the doctor's signature that would restore my autonomy.

Leaving the New York Hospital is a festive event. The spacious lobby is an art deco masterpiece. Gleaming silver arches stretch toward the sky. The marble floors, embedded with commemorative medallions, support people from all over the world. They walk swiftly through the revolving doors or sit in the lobby graced with beautiful plants to await their loved ones. After Tim wheeled me down to the first floor, I reveled in the walk through the revolving doors to freedom and fresh air. My trip home was an initiation. Everything shimmering in the afternoon heat felt brand new. I was the city whizzing past my window. I observed it and became it at once, relishing this ability to savor everything with my senses. The cloistered hospital environment had been like a convent with its ordered daily routine. Arriving at this heightened awareness was almost worth the ordeal. I wanted to bottle it like a fragrance and keep it forever.

XII.

An Exalted Master

Over the years, I had established myself as a violinist, but still the financial picture looked bleak. I applied for unemployment to make it through the slow times. The unemployment office, located in Washington Heights, was housed in one mammoth room painted a dingy, nondescript blue. The ceiling had Styrofoam panels punched with tiny holes that looked like the surface of the moon. Fluorescent lighting gave the space a macabre cast. In the center, standing in line, were several hundred irate people. Many were writers, actors, dancers or musicians. Others were able-bodied men who seemed happy to be on the government dole. Applying for a claim was made as difficult as possible by inefficient government employees with an attitude. I found the experience saddening and wished I could be anywhere else.

To pass the time, I retrieved a folder of books that I had brought to amuse myself. A self-help catalogue caught my eye. *There, on the second page, was a picture of a young man named Daniel. He was standing in a wheat field dressed in a simple white shirt and jeans. My gaze moved to his face. I could not take my eyes off him. What an attractive man, I was thinking when, suddenly, a golden halo formed around his head. It moved down the page, traveling directly toward me, and disappeared. I rubbed my eyes. I must be seeing things! I thought. Yet, the golden halo had been as real as my dismal surroundings. This beautiful halo had reached out to me. I trusted this vision. Daniel was an Enlightened Master with magnetism great enough to guide me to him.*

Eagerly I explored the catalogue. The tapes promised a course in spiritual mastery based on Daniel's understandings. Normally I would have passed up such an opportunity as another program I could not afford, but this was different. Here was proof, through my vision, that Daniel was seeking me to be his student! I returned to Daniel's image hoping to see the halo, but this time I saw nothing. Even so, I was determined to learn the source of this man's power.

I dug through my meager finances to order his tapes, and they finally arrived. I was not disappointed. After an inner quest that had lasted for years, Daniel had formulated a system for self-mastery in which he recommended cleansing oneself from 'lower vibrations'. Entering a guided meditation state and using a hypnotic technique could erase feelings of anger, guilt, hatred and fear. He warned that these strong emotions are very powerful and often manifest themselves by allowing the event most feared into one's life.

His technique for 'mental clearing', as he termed it, was extremely effective. This method could release distasteful events, and possibly disease from my life. Daniel taught that physical healing occurred by tapping into the 'ethers' around us, or the kundalini energy that exists everywhere in space. A channeling of that energy could effect a healing. I was thrilled. Here were the tools to rid myself of lupus forever. Knowing about a healing and creating one were two different things, however. I searched for practical applications and found that concentration was essential. By holding an image of healing strong enough, it manifested in an instant, as in Jesus Christ's miraculous accomplishments. Daniel taught that the skill of healing could be learned. This gave me hope for the future. I vowed to learn the creative power of healing.

We are all subject to vast universal laws, whether we choose to acknowledge them or not. Daniel maintained that finding these laws and working with them enables us to minimize accidents, sickness or poverty and become a creator of life rather than a hapless spectator.

A plan was emerging. I would unearth the causes of my disease by digging into my subconscious mind where fears and guilts were stored. However, how much of a change could I effect? I had reached the conclusion that lupus was brought on by negative emotions which I had turned inward and allowed to manifest as illness.

Daniel explained that, in order to align oneself with universal laws one must practice positive speech and control all thoughts. I practiced the latter, but the former was going to be difficult. People in our culture often lapse into judgmental thinking. At times I succumbed to an 'us against them' approach, believing that my way was superior. Daniel was asking me, instead, to assume the kindest thoughts towards others. This formula would transmute karma through the power of love. Transmutation was a new concept for me. Through transmutation, lower emotions such as fear, guilt and anger changed through the power of love.

For many years, I rejected the concept of healing love because I assumed that the church took responsibility. Jesus was the healer. Not understanding the power of this intermediary, I felt ineffectual. My forays into eastern religion had divested me of the mandate to feel guilty about sin. Now I realized that the healing love of which Jesus spoke is a tangible force through the laws of transmutation—a cleansing of the lower emotions through love. Love is the law of the Universe. The creative fiat is love. Plants, animals and humans "live and have their being" through love. To direct the love force with the aim of healing would elevate one to a state of grace. It seemed clear that the mastery of this force could accomplish miracles.

I was discovering the tools that would enable me to direct the power of love. I had attracted pain and physical crises into my life. These were a means of spiritual awakening which could bring me to a higher level of mastery.

I had already learned much through my search for a cure. Daniel advised learning our lessons through wisdom rather than woe. I wondered if this was possible. To dwell in the higher dimensions without pain was an enticing concept. Though I had not evolved to this lofty level yet, it was becoming apparent that habitual thought patterns did indeed play a large part in the formation of my disease. I was excited to discover that I could change the distorted, destructive thoughts that had harmed my body. Through changing these erroneous thoughts on a deep subconscious level, I might release the need for lupus.

We live in the dense vibration of the physical universe. Daniel claimed, as did Edgar Cayce, that there are other, finer dimensions, which vibrate at faster rates. Scientists have shown that plants possess an aura, or an energy field, which surrounds them. I have seen this myself. One evening I cut a leaf from a plant and saw its outline although it was no longer there. This phantom leaf was the aura, or energy field, around the leaf. Because these higher vibrations are usually invisible, most people cannot see auras. Nevertheless, we all possess them.

Another important concept is gratitude. Though, of course, I had been tutored in gratitude from earliest Sunday school, Daniel stressed that frequency and depth of emotion were important. How many times had I taken the bounty in my life for granted! I began to say a small prayer of thanks, to make it a habit, so that each time I became aware of another blessing it was acknowledged. My illness had given me a capacity for gratitude forged through the loss of these blessings. Indeed, an inability to feel deep gratitude often had been the impetus for attraction of illness into my life. Yet, I would learn the real meaning of this concept soon enough.

XIII.

First Kidney Involvement

By that November of 1985, I found myself in The Hospital for Special Surgery again. My kidneys, affected by the onslaughts of pneumonia, meningitis and three hospital stays, were leaking protein. I was now diagnosed with lupus nephritis, or lupus attacking the kidneys. Dr. Christian prescribed 60 milligrams of prednisone. Always aware of my resistance, he admonished me to stay on the drug. It seemed simple. I would take prednisone and the disease would go away. However, I was a different person physically, mentally and emotionally under its influence. Again, my face 'mooned' and my body swelled up. I experienced the familiar mood swings.

I had never joined a lupus support group because the interaction required was too painful. If I had attended, I might have seen those who suffered from kidney failure and this might have served as a further inspiration to maintain my health.

However, shored up with spiritual knowledge, I faced this latest challenge with equanimity. Fortunately a kidney biopsy showed little damage and I was sent home after a few days. I was so ashamed of my strange appearance that I found it very difficult to face my colleagues. In addition, the emotional fragility created by the drug increased my self-consciousness.

I accepted a church performance in Brooklyn Heights. On the day of the first rehearsal, I went shopping for clothes that would hide my huge stomach. I found a woman's large size store on Broadway and bought some shapeless black clothing. After the rehearsal, an old friend walked me to the subway.

"How have you been, Marilyn?" Ron asked as we passed restored brownstones and well-tended gardens.

"Oh, just fine," I said hastily, struggling to keep up with him on the narrow sidewalk. Ron and I had known each other since Aspen. I felt like a truck in my large green-and-white sweatshirt, but he seemed not to notice. I was grateful for his tact, surmising that the steroids had exaggerated my discomfort.

A clarinetist hired me to perform with my string quartet in Brooklyn. It was a nice program of Haydn and Mozart. During our two weeks of rehearsal, I grew progressively larger. I felt a cloying fear for my condition, but I kept this to myself. The night of the concert I warmed up in front of a mirror. My new dress made me look like a bat, but it concealed my burgeoning stomach effectively. It was a heavy burden to keep these fears to myself, but I could not confide in my colleagues. They would not understand my concern for the future or the mood swings that I tried so desperately to conceal. I felt that my illness was a deeply personal issue. I was never tempted to confide my fears for the future to anyone but Tim. In spite of my misery, the concert was a success.

I fled to my parents for Thanksgiving. Surely, they would take care of me without judgment. I was wrong. My loved ones were shocked at the swift change that the high dosage of cortisone had wrought. My hair had again fallen out, so I cut it short. There was a flurry of comment on my new look.

"Marl, I love your haircut!" Mother exclaimed. "You look just like Angela—you know, the one on television?"

"No I don't, Mother," I muttered.

"You do, Marl. It's very becoming."

She was trying to be tactful, but I felt repulsive. I had not chosen this look; it had chosen me! Yet, here was Mother, in far worse shape than I was. After she developed emphysema, it was torture to be around her, to watch her struggle for each breath. The braces were gone, but her hands were permanently drawn inward. Mother would never play again. I thought of the joy her skilled hands had brought others, and I cried. Her skin was very thin and she bruised easily. When she bumped into anything, her skin tore. Currently she was nursing a wound she had gotten when she collided with the dishwasher that had become infected.

I commiserated with Mother, but the haven I sought was not there. Her similar concerns were discomfiting, a painful reminder of my possible fate. I redoubled my spiritual efforts to get at the cause of this dis-ease. Unfortunately, the steroids made meditation difficult. Without this release, it was more difficult to gain control of my emotions. Often I would feel as if I had just consumed ten cups of coffee. I still believed that the sickness I was experiencing was formed before the steroid treatment arrested it. However, once it was in full swing, I could not use spiritual methods for its serious treatment. The cortisone made these methods impossible, but I had to admit that I could not face these crises alone.

When I was a child, my father was often dominant. I sometimes found it difficult to speak up. Now my endless health crises continued to foster that same sense of failure.

I returned to New York. That fall I had enrolled in a writing correspondence course. One frigid afternoon in December I was researching at the New York Public Library when I had a sudden panic attack. The marble walls began to close in on me. I wanted to scream. Gathering my papers, I hastened out of the library and searched for a cab, but no one would stop for me. By the time I arrived home, I was nauseous and unbalanced. The entire experience was profoundly disturbing. I was on sensory overload, trying to accomplish too much. I had not even begun a career in free-lance article writing. All of my time and energy was devoted to playing the violin. This wall of resistance given as real physical symptoms was a warning for me to back off, but I should have paid more attention to the real message underneath my reactions.

I played concertmaster for *Madame Butterfly* with a small orchestra in Westchester. It was a challenge I relished. The masterpiece is one of the most beautiful works in the repertoire. I studied the score and prepared my part with care. During the performance, in an important solo, I came perilously close to fainting. Though I quickly recovered, this indicated that something was very wrong. These signals, and the deep sense of discomfort they engendered, should have been signposts. Instead, I ignored them and continued with my life as best I could. I did not realize that they were clues indicating that I was about to give up.

Fall has always been my favorite season, possibly because it is the time of my birth. Trees flash their colors and we taste the first evening coolness in the air. This particular fall and winter I could not quite get started. I developed a fear bordering on panic that my health would again careen out of control. With a sigh of relief, I bade the year farewell. I had finished it without mishap and managed to stay out of the hospital. As the New Year began, I was feeling healthy and enjoying a full career, and I was full of hope that my problems were behind me.

As I traveled from stage to stage, I marveled at the fact that the personnel remained remarkably the same. These groups of people were my colleagues. I had performed with many of them from my first professional contract at the Eastern Music Festival to Aspen, to Iceland— throughout a professional life of almost fifteen years. One morning, arriving at the last minute for a rehearsal with the Queens Symphony, I lingered backstage to watch the musicians warm up. *In an instant, the musicians on-stage were transformed into a brilliant, radiating white light. Each was a tiny star, blazing in its own right. I gasped. Here was a small galaxy, preparing to make music. That these colleagues, my soulmates with whom I shared the pleasure of music-making, would be revealed to me in such a way filled me with joy. I felt bathed in love for each one of them.*

Meanwhile, back on the earth plane, my daily 60-milligram dosage of prednisone had made me almost unrecognizable. Connie, a friend who had not seen me since the Milstein Master Class several years earlier, was shocked at my appearance. "What happened to you?" she asked bluntly as we were sitting down to play.

"Uh, I've been taking a large dose of cortisone. It changes my appearance."

"Oh."

My statement seemed to have no impact. We shared a stand for the tremendously difficult *Cappriccio* by Richard Strauss. Her comment, fueled by the drug, inflamed me. Each comment, mannerism, or mark she made on the music set me on edge. My emotionalism, coupled with the fact that I appeared to be an entirely different person, made the work a grueling ordeal.

Another group started rehearsals a few days later. Again, spurred on by the drug, I could hardly control my comments. Morris, the conductor, seemed determined to prevent us from making music.

"Play louder at bar 53," he said, singing the phrase as he wanted it.

"Sure, we could do that if you'd conduct it that way," I muttered under my breath, glowering. At the next rendition of bar 53, I deliberately exaggerated his request. He looked at me disapprovingly, though he did not comment. I glowered back. His lame conducting was certainly something I could handle if I had been feeling normal, but I was feeling decidedly on edge and out of control.

I obligated myself to play second violin in a string quartet. We were to play the Ravel Quartet, a masterpiece, at a church in Washington Heights. Though this was a more intimate setting, I was still self-conscious about my appearance. Again, I kept my fears to myself, but it was sometimes a hardship to bear my illness and uncertainty for the future alone. A legitimate reason for discretion was that my colleagues might wonder if I had lost my capacity to perform. Though a musician is not an actor, his body is on display when he performs. A certain amount of image is necessary. Musicians run from rehearsal to concert, often traveling to other states or countries, grabbing meals when they can. This does not leave a lot of time for make-up and beauty appointments. My friends in the string quartet certainly did not care how I looked, but I felt they were simply being tactful. Though the concert came and went uneventfully, I realized that the drug had again exacerbated my discomfort.

I was becoming impatient with the merry-go-round cortisone cycle and its uncertain conclusions. Therefore, I worked earnestly to use my spiritual principles, always searching for new keys to unlock the doorway to health. A book called *You Can Heal Your Life*, by Louise Hay, gave me another piece to the puzzle. She maintained that lupus patients feel guilt and a need for punishment. This inner belief creates pain in their bodies. Ms. Hay had cured herself of cancer, an achievement that offered dramatic proof of the efficacy of her methods. I began to state her affirmations daily and to look even deeper within myself to weed out errant thoughts. Consequently, I was able—again, under Dr. Christian's supervision—to taper the prednisone, and my appearance slowly returned to normal.

Amidst these discoveries, my mother again went to the National Institute of Health in Maryland. As her recovery progressed, she began to notice other patients and their problems. One night she called me with this story:

"I had been at the N. I. H. for two months when, late one night, a young girl was admitted. She was only twenty-six years old, an attractive newscaster embarking upon a promising career. Having driven all day and into the night, she arrived at the N.I.H. bloated and weak. She had lupus nephritis but could not believe the diagnosis. She could beat it and succeed, just as she did with everything in her life. She maintained her obligations as if nothing was happening, refusing to take her medication. This worked for awhile until the nephritis became strong within her. She did not eat but kept putting on weight. Her trip to the N.I.H. was an attempt to salvage a situation that had gotten out of control. She died that night."

Mother's cautionary tale should have warned me. Nevertheless, I was feeling good that summer. Using Daniel's tapes and meditating on the healing power of love, I regained my health. Two years passed. During the summer of 1987, I played concertmaster briefly for the Glimmerglass Opera's first season in their new home in Cooperstown. Dad loaned me his car and I drove it from Weems to upstate New York. I returned the car to Weems. After my sojourn upstate, I looked forward to revisiting the waterfront property I had loved every summer as a child. Like Mother, I felt cleansed and replenished near this special body of water. Each morning I sat in meditation on the carpeted floor of the green-and-yellow guest bedroom that Mother had decorated in her unique style.

Feeling powerless against the accelerating nature of her condition, I wondered if I might contribute to her healing by accessing the spiritual silence of meditation. Though I was not a spiritual healer, I had learned, through Daniel's tapes, that the *kundalini* energy inherent in all space could effect a healing. I realized that a miraculous healing could happen only with great concentration, and that the subject must be receptive.

I was not sure that Mother would be completely amenable, so I decided to heal her on my own. She was not against my meditative practices; she just did not understand them. Mother enjoyed the social life of the church, but I did not see her pray in earnest until she was seriously ill. I knew that she would not object if I tried to make her situation better, so I envisioned her surrounded by a white light of protection and a blue healing light. I sought to remove her pain with all the concentration I could muster. Though I attempted this numerous times, picturing her in complete health, I failed. It was possible that my loving efforts brought her some relief. However, my mother's condition had been a long time forming. Moreover, as with my failed attempt to heal by faith in the midst of a flare, my regenerative powers would need to be great to succeed. I flew back to my apartment in the city, feeling that my healing efforts were ineffectual. A few weeks later, I got a call from Dad.

"Marilyn, you'd better come. Mom is not doing well."

"What is it, Dad?"

"She had an episode. They rushed her to Rappahannock General where they put her on a respirator." He sighed. "It looks as though we might have to make a decision."

I flew down home. Bob and Jeff were already there when I arrived, gathered around her bed. I was shocked to see her hooked up to the respirator. Without her thick glasses, she could barely see us. Nevertheless, she greeted me with a smile. We stayed at her side for days, willing her to beat this latest setback. However, we knew it was impossible. There had been too many drugs, too many years of slow deterioration.

With each visit the same hopeless state of affairs continued until Mother indicated that she wished to be taken off the respirator. The other option, a tracheotomy, would be a risk in her perilous condition. Dad, Bob, Jeff and I agonized over this decision. Though we were afraid it would mean certain death, we hoped that Mother could rally and win the battle.

On Labor Day, she struggled a full twenty-four hours for her final breaths. Her gray-green eyes darted back and forth helplessly and I held her skeletal hand in mine, encouraging her to fight. It was the most difficult thing I have ever had to do. I tried to be strong but I did not want her to go. Finally, her hand went limp. The struggle was over.

XIV.

Second Nephritis

During the two years that I enjoyed good health I worked with Daniel's tapes and cleared myself of many emotions that needed to be eradicated in order to be free. This was a long process. Finding childhood fears and guilts in my subconscious during meditation, I erased them slowly through forgiveness. I had come a long way in understanding the causes of my illness. However, slowly, insidiously, I became complacent. I neglected my spiritual practices of meditation, gratitude, and thought control. For many living without the scourge of lupus, this relaxation from the regimen would have no effect. For me it was disastrous.

By November of 1988 I had known for several months that something was wrong with me, but I was not anxious to repeat my experience with lupus nephritis. When I finally admitted to Tim that I was not feeling well, he insisted that I contact Dr. Christian. I was certain that Dr. Christian would prescribe cortisone. Ever hopeful that I could somehow reverse the process, I put off making the call.

Meanwhile, I dragged myself to rehearsals and concerts. I was going through the motions, acting out my life, as if someone else was drawing the bow across the strings. Many of my performances paid poorly. I felt taken advantage of and resentful. I embedded this indignation deep inside. Soon it would manifest as a full-blown lupus flare. I should have known better. I was miserable in our dingy apartment. Our drab bedroom faced

West 94th Street, a block where drug deals were made twenty-four hours a day. Gangs of small Latino Americans partied under our window late into the night. Car alarms went off every hour. It was impossible to get a sound night's sleep.

My condition was worsening, and still I would try anything but cortisone. Trina Wells, a violinist friend, suggested that we attend a faith-healing seminar. She met me on the subway and we traveled to the plant district in lower Manhattan. Tall palms, marginatas and sheflera lined the streets as we made our way to the dance studio for the seminar. It was like walking through a tropical garden. At the studio, an expectant crowd of a dozen people greeted us.

The 'healer' was short. One leg was longer than the other was, and he wore a platform shoe. His wife wore a stunning green dress reminiscent of the 50's, her flaming red hair neatly done up in a bouffant. Intrigued by the strange pair, I paid $250 for the entrance fee. After the introductory lecture I was convinced to spend a few hundred more based on testimony of customers whom I later conjectured were planted in the audience.

Trina meant well. She thought she was helping me overcome my lupus problem. We discussed New Age philosophies and diet. When I confided that I had recently lacked energy, she offered to give me a 'healing' which involved realigning me. After it was over, I felt nothing other than my usual lack of energy. Though I knew the consequences of seeking alternative cures in a crisis, I consoled myself with the supposition that I was not in a crisis. Yet.

I found myself purchasing materials for the course. The 'remote healer' advocated clapping to remove evil spirits around the house. It seemed ridiculous, but the pair was very convincing. After the seminar I was instructed to participate in 'remote faith healings', since this man lived in the Southwest. Though the fluid retention in my legs had grown alarmingly evident, I trusted him and persevered with his treatments, which were simply to drink cider vinegar. Optimistically I participated in 'remote' treatments over a period of ten weeks while my condition steadily deteriorated. I paid this charlatan $200 for an irreversible slide downwards. Tim was furious. Didn't I realize that my condition was worsening?

I knew in my heart that I had created another lupus flare, but I could not face the cortisone. I persisted in the 'treatments' hoping that this man would lift the lupus curse. I was foolish to place my trust in someone that I barely knew. The lupus flare was fashioned through months and years of erroneous thinking and neglectful behavior. It was not going to go away so easily. Yet, the irrational part of me believed that lupus was a curse. Even so, it was becoming obvious that cider vinegar was not going to lift this scourge from my body.

Though I was still reluctant to visit Dr. Christian, Tim finally forced me to make an appointment. After some bloodwork, we met Dr. Christian outside the laboratory where my worst fears were confirmed. "You're having a flare, Marilyn," the handsome doctor towered over me. "I want you to start taking thirty milligrams of prednisone immediately."

"Every other day?" I asked hopefully.

"No. Every day." My heart sank. Although my ankles were thickening with retained fluid, a sure sign that my kidneys were not working, this edict brought out my fighting spirit. I still was not ready to give up. I took the prednisone, but continued my remote treatments secretly.

Our fourth wedding anniversary passed. Tim and I wanted to work together so we decided to create a chamber group for Young Audiences. This booking agency promoted concerts in the New York City Public Schools. We asked a cellist friend, Yari Bond, to join us, and composed a script that interspersed jazz, Michael Jackson, Vivaldi, and Rachmaninoff.

After composing the script and rehearsing it, we auditioned for the Young Audiences agency. We wore black jeans, black shirts and colorful thin satin ties. I thought we looked great.

On the day of our audition, I stood in silhouette in our warm-up room. "You're too thin," Tim commented.

"No, I'm not. I like the way I look," I retorted.

"You're not eating right, Marilyn," Tim frowned.

"Okay. I'll eat more," I said to placate him. Actually, I enjoyed my appearance. Always striving to attain thinness, I felt that I had almost reached my goal. I ignored my husband's comment.

The audition went well and we joined the roster of Young Audience artists. However, our first performance was a shock. In the months since the audition, my condition had deteriorated so drastically that I could barely walk to the second floor of our first school. I would sing Rachmaninoff's *Vocalise* in our program. However, I barely made it through a phrase over the voices of the children in the audience. After stumbling through two performances that morning I canceled the remaining shows, hired a substitute, and called Dr. Christian that afternoon. He suggested that I wait until the next week to enter the hospital. I agreed, though I feared that stepping across its threshold would relinquish control of my life. I did not realize to what extent this would soon become true.

Over the weekend of December 3rd and the subsequent weekend of December 10th, 1988, I was to perform the operetta *Orpheus in the Underworld* by Offenbach with the Village Light Opera Company. Walking was difficult due to the swelling in my ankles. Nevertheless, I dragged myself downtown to each performance. One evening I decided to exit the subway at the 34th Street stop. As I made my way along the urine-soaked cement with the homeless sprawled around me, my spirit shriveled. I was so tired, yet these people were in worse shape than I was. I trudged up the stairway to 32nd Street, planning to walk a few blocks to 28th. The station was deserted with the exception of three men lurking at the top of the stairs. I was terrified—the men had seen me. To flee would invite disaster. Bravely I continued, looking straight ahead. Fortunately, the men did not bother me.

Orpheus in the Underworld is etched on my soul laced with the panic it evokes. I have played many pieces of music. Some are joyous, some profound, and some sad. In particularly emotional times, music mingles with life like blood with tears. Ron Noll, a sincere and dedicated musician, directs the Village Light Opera Company. I felt a camaraderie with Ron, a mutual respect. However, for this series of performances I felt completely apart. I was living a separate reality which Ron and my other colleagues could not begin to comprehend.

The performance became a mirror for my soul, which was opposite to the joy inherent in the music. I made myself appear at the productions only to satisfy my obligations. I was miserable, alone in an unhappy world of my own making. My anger stemmed from my feelings of helplessness. Playing this lighthearted music seemed so incongruous when I was facing a grievous illness.

That weekend my brother Bob visited. He was the drummer of a band that was making a demo record at a New York studio. He was excited, of course, and did not notice my diminished condition. He had never been to visit me before, and I was hoping for happier circumstances. On the morning of his departure, I made him bacon and eggs. It was almost like old times. As we sat at the breakfast table, I could barely hold back the tears. I felt so helpless and frightened. However, Bob was unaware of my state of mind. He, like everyone else, was living his own life. Somehow, I thought my brother would feel more sympathy. Maybe I was wishing he could rescue me.

Monday morning, December 11, arrived and with it the inevitability of my promise to Dr. Christian. I kissed our cats good-bye and packed a few belongings. Tim and I took a cab to the Hospital for Special Surgery. The lobby was glaring with a fluorescent light as raw as my visceral awareness. New patients filled out forms and went upstairs to their beds. I waited. It seemed strange to be waiting. The lobby looked like a hotel, but we were not waiting for a pleasant place to rest our heads after a day of fun and travel. We were waiting to sign our lives over to an uncertain conclusion. I wondered who had terminal diseases and would not be leaving the hospital alive, who would lose limbs or organs, and who would be the lucky ones, treated for minor problems from which they would soon recover. The fear and helplessness that imbued the faces of those around me transmitted their frenetic awareness. I felt like a condemned woman going to the guillotine.

After hours of waiting, I settled into my bed. Dr. Christian prescribed intravenous glucose and prednisone and my condition immediately declined. I had held my finger in the dam as long as I could. A strange metallic taste killed my appetite. I ate virtually nothing yet kept gaining weight, and in a few days I ballooned to 160 pounds. The fluid that I gained congregated near my lungs, making it almost impossible to breathe. I also developed a severe, splitting headache, like a migraine or a hangover that never went away.

Doctor Christian visited me once or twice daily with several students. It seemed the same questions were asked by each of the numerous faces thrust into mine. Hoping for a swift return to my career, I was dismayed at the speed with which I was slipping past the decisive point. From my hospital bed, I cancelled Christmas performances of Bach's *Saint John Passion* and Mozart's *Magic Flute*, which I had been eagerly anticipating. The *Saint John Passion* is a long, profound work with orchestra, choir and solo singers. I had performed it once before but I was again eager to journey through this profound music of faith with the great master Bach. The *Magic Flute* is great fun. I was anticipating the challenge of learning the first violin part to this beautiful piece. Instead, day melted into miserable day as I slid down my spiral of sickness.

Finally, Dr. Christian became alarmed that my kidneys were failing and ordered pulse therapy. Although I was terrified, I realized that this shock treatment might chase the lupus away and give my kidneys a chance to recover. Then I began to produce antibodies against myself, and hemolytic anemia joined my congregation of illnesses. Dr. Christian ordered transfusions, but I made antibodies against them too. In addition, I had picked up a virulent strain of hospital bacteria. My fever escalated and I began to hallucinate. Dr. Christian became concerned that I would not survive. The pulse therapy had not worked and breathing was a terrifying struggle. We were running out of alternatives.

Now I would enter a phase that would change my life forever. In this distorted world, I lurked in the shadows. Here in the murky recesses of my new life underwater, everyone spoke without sound or meaning. The surface, where healthy people lived, was a place where my admission pass had just run out.

XV.

Hemodialysis

Doctor Christian had administered every treatment in his arsenal. The pulse therapy should have worked, considering my past response to megadoses of cortisone. Instead I retained the glucose and my body continued to swell. The metallic taste never left my mouth and the toxins kept accumulating. My headache was a continual agony, but at least the hemolytic anemia reversed with the transfusions, and the mysterious virus was under control through antibiotics.

The torturous pulse therapy, finally at an end, had been a barbaric experience. The drug was responsible for the flights of hallucination that threatened to seize my consciousness permanently. I had hung on with all my will, determined to ride the wave of illusion through to reality.

Now, on Christmas Day, 1988, I was stable enough to be dialyzed. Dr. Christian continued to visit my bedside with punctual professionalism, but I sensed his withdrawal. With the order of dialysis, he had reluctantly allowed me to take the first step toward a process that would be my brutal master in the years to come. No longer just a lupus patient, I was now a victim of catastrophic kidney failure. The magnitude of his decision was not immediately apparent, but it would soon become abundantly clear.

Dr. Christian had fought gallantly by my side. He had weighed the portentious decision with his usual care. He must have seen many lupus patients succumb to kidney attacks. Dr. Christian knew my independent spirit. Throughout the past few years, his prescription of cortisone had been a constant battle between us, but he was always willing to listen to me. His decision to dialyze me was devastating but this was my only chance for survival.

Finally, the moment arrived. A nurse moved me to a stretcher and left me at the nurse's station with my chart on my stomach. I struggled for air and squinted at the bright lights. After a long wait, a page and her girlfriend whisked me through the maze of subterranean caverns connecting the Hospital for Special Surgery to the New York Hospital. Feeling like an invisible cargo to be transported, I peeked up at them. Their staccato conversation punctuated our journey. I did not understand what they were saying, but still I listened curiously. I envied them. They were not facing a life of dependence. Their concerns were how to do their hair or what to have for dinner that night.

Suddenly, the ceiling whizzing past me faded from my consciousness and I was at the bottom of a large hole. It was a soggy day, dark and sad. Doctors, nurses and pages stood on the ground above, peering down at me. The dialysis decree had thrown me deeper into this gaping pit. I felt vulnerable at the mercy of these strangers. The gap between healthy people and me had suddenly widened.

My awareness shifted back to the present reality. After our tour of the catacombs in the New York Hospital, the talkative page and her girlfriend went on their merry way. I found myself in an enormous room full of machines. The walls had recently been painted a light peach. There were no other patients. They had opened it especially for me! M-2, the gleaming catastrophic dialysis center of the New York Hospital, was not normally open on Christmas day. If I had not been feeling so wretched, I would have been impressed.

A resident approached my stretcher.

"Hi. I'm Dr. Spynapidoros," he smiled down at me, touching my arm gently. "We are going to dialyze you," he explained. "First, I'll insert this needle in your groin." He brandished one of the largest needles I had ever seen.

"You will be anesthetized locally to reduce the pain. Then, we will insert a catheter in the large vein in your leg. This will be the access route as the machine takes the blood out of your body, cleanses it, and replaces it. We'll remove excess fluid, but slowly, a few pounds at a time."

I was terrified at the prospect of this horrifying procedure. I felt so small; my swollen body dwarfed in the cavernous room. Yet, without hesitation, I gritted my teeth and replied, "This is the answer to my prayers." I was ready for anything that would remove the death toxins.

Donning rubber gloves, he covered my groin area with a blue paper with a circular hole in its center. He then placed an assortment of surgical instruments on the paper. Opening the sterile packet, he removed a wooden wand with a betadyne solution, a copper-colored substance, soaked through a cotton tip. With the wand, he rubbed my right groin in a circular motion. Then he brandished another needle, not nearly as large as the first one, with which he inserted lydocane into my vein. As I was waiting for the anesthesia to take effect, he produced the larger needle that located the femoral vein. Because of the amount of fluid I retained, the vein was not easy to locate at first stick. After the shock of this invasive procedure, the prospect of bracing myself for more pain took my breath away. Fortunately, the young doctor performed efficiently. I endured.

He removed a tube from another sterile package. This catheter, a thin, rubber implement, was to be inserted inside my vein! Mercifully, the process was over quickly. I held my breath, grateful that the anesthesia had numbed my feeling, but terrified at this assault on my body.

The catheter was inserted down my leg.

"Don't move for the next four hours," Dr. Spynapidoros warned. "If you do, you risk a blood clot and death."

I made a small motion resembling a nod, too frightened to move my head. The dialysis nurse produced two sets of plastic tubes. One set led to the dialysis machine. The other led away from the machine and back into my groin. The blood was slowly pumped out of my body, then replaced. My first dialysis machine was computerized. A complicated series of numbers appeared as the process progressed. I watched in horror as the clear tubes took on the deep red hue of my own lifeblood.

The head nurse, Ms. Perricone, came to open the dialysis unit. She recommended that I take a Valium to soften the shock. "We think this may ease your distress on the first dialysis," she said, smiling.

"Uh, okay," I managed. I had never taken a Valium before. Though it was obvious that my first dialysis would be traumatic, I was totally unprepared for the effect of the drug.

Once I was hooked up to the machine, the torturous process of lying entirely still while my blood was pumped into the cleansing machine and out again began. Ms. Perricone conversed with Dr. Spynapidoros in an abrasive voice that my poisoned senses amplified. I wanted to scream, "Shut up!" but was unable to speak.

Two hours into the procedure, Nureyev appeared to me as a pixie in a butterfly costume. In spite of the hallucination, I held on, trying to believe that this process would dig me out of the pit that continued to float through my consciousness. Surrender was not an option.

Awakening from my lightheaded Valium dream, I found myself in a strange nether world in which the edges of my awareness softened. The light in the room took on a strange yellow hue. My body felt like wet clay. Helplessly I careened through a winding tunnel that sucked me down, knocking out my wind. I was powerless to direct its outcome. The combination of my traumatic first dialysis experience, pulse steroid therapy, nephritis, lack of sleep and anemia had taken its effect. I was adrift in a sea of hallucination, terrified at my loss of control. This mental and emotional chaos was more frightening than physical agony.

After an interminable three-and-a-half hours spent totally still, a small Fillipino nurse appeared at my bedside. "It's almost over," she smiled.

I held my breath as the nurse removed the snakelike catheter with amazing speed. Immediately thereafter, she thrust her entire weight in finger pressure on the wound at my groin for a full fifteen minutes. Next, she placed a ten-pound sandbag over the point of entry to insure that the chasm they had created would not spurt. I was utterly spent. I felt violated, as if an oncoming vehicle had hit me and left me in the road for dead. I noticed the nurses expressing sympathy.

"Poor thing," one of them frowned. "She's been through it."

The two nurses lifted me from the dialysis bed onto a plastic implement resembling a surfboard. Limply ensconced again on my stretcher, I was deposited in a corner with my chart on my stomach. Another forty-five minutes passed until the page arrived, during which my consciousness faded in and out of focus. Through a haze of pain, I dimly realized that I had crossed a line. It was, actually, a momentous occasion. I had survived my first dialysis treatment. This was an appropriate time to mourn for my life of health and vitality. I was an invalid now, completely dependent on this severe procedure for survival. Tears streaked my face as I fought despair. I would soon enter a world unlike any I had ever known. The joyous light of music was gone, the sun of my life eclipsed. My life would now consist of severe anemia and its attendant crushing fatigue, as well as obeisance to this harsh procedure for a base level of survival.

After my first dialysis experience, I was expected to become accustomed to the routine. Dialysis treatments occurred once every two days. Mercifully, the excess fluid dropped off slowly with the help of these marvelous machines. Now that I was officially a victim of catastrophic kidney failure, the dreaded trip to M-2 was always a source of terror. As an inpatient, my hours were flexible. My stretcher was wheeled in late at night or early in the morning, when I could be fit into their crowded schedule.

As the catastrophic dialysis center of the New York Hospital, the staff at M-2 treats an assortment of patients as ill as I had become. Though many were dialysis veterans, there were also neophytes like me. On one evening, a young man came in to experience his first dialysis stick. He was tall and blonde with horn-rimmed glasses, obviously from a wealthy family. I surmised he was about twenty years old.

"No!" he screamed, as the needle entered his groin. "I don't need this! Get me out of here! Let me go!" His mother tried to calm him, without success. I empathized. My first treatment was a painfully recent memory. I would have screamed, too, if I could have.

Another regular customer at M-2 was a slight man bearing the yellowish caste of a dialysis veteran. A thick rubber tube for access to the machine looped in a half-circle outside his neck. I was appalled at the risk such a tube represented. With a single slip, a lethal antibody could enter the artery and spread throughout the system. His small body was slumped in the wheelchair. I found later that he had diabetes, a common twin to kidney failure.

A young girl who was battling an extreme bout with lupus came by during my shift. She had a moon face, most of her brown hair was gone, and she was severely bloated.

I cannot look that bad, I thought, but I had little perspective. Perhaps we were identical.

I soon became familiar with the routine. Patients' last names were posted on a chalkboard and rearranged. I recognized the first and second year interns who performed the surgery of inserting the catheters. It was embarrassing for young men to be sticking needles in my groin, so I preferred the women. Unfortunately, they were in the minority. Gossip among patients revealed some doctors to be notoriously bad 'stickers'. This meant that they were compelled to repeat the painful femoral process. It was not a preferred state of affairs. I noticed that women increasingly populated the medical profession. Women were also trained in impartial observance, but they seemed to have an intuitive empathy lacking in men. At this vulnerable time, as I grappled with the issues of machine dependence and invalidism, I wished that any medical professional would lend a hand of caring compassion. Yet, the doctors in M-2 who treated me all seemed curiously detached.

They're sleep-deprived and overworked, I thought. Obviously, their distance was also self-protective. Empathizing with the sickness of each patient would make it impossible for him or her to face the suffering. Still, I wondered if they noted that I was a fellow human attempting to endure an extreme state of crisis with dignity. On the other hand, did their training shift their vision to a hospital chart with a set of symptoms?

After my first dialysis, Dr. John Sullivan became my kidney specialist. Here was a most empathetic doctor. Dr. Sullivan had the courage to care. He suffered a little with every patient. His loving concern gave me hope that, indeed, there is a place where the sympathetic nerve has not been severed. His devotion to the welfare of his patients gave him heroic stature. Certainly, there are many selfless physicians whose burning concern is the well being of their patients, but I know of none with the grace and passion of Dr. Sullivan. This was apparent from the beginning of our association, though at first my weakened state blocked the realization.

I saw Dr. Christian less now. Lupus had done its worst. Now I would face the ravages in its wake. Dr. Christian had pulled me through discoid lupus and spinal meningitis and averted a kidney failure as long as possible. Now with each visit there was an unbridgeable chasm forming between us. His professional dedication was unimpeachable. I had no doubt that he was concerned for my welfare and I felt guilty for fighting with him so often and challenging his medical advice. I believe that lupus patients often possess helplessness along with a subconscious wish for punishment. Through years of inner evaluation, I had discovered that guilt plays an important role in the formation of a flare. The symptoms' command for attention allows for an abdication of responsibility. My lack of self-esteem had gotten me a respite from adult commitments. I would not discover how to liberate myself from this state until much later. Now, as kidney failure commanded my attention, I would move away from Dr. Christian.

My new life of machine dependency was like existing in a cage. No one outside could understand what it was like inside my cage of dialysis. One day a flutist colleague of Tim's came to visit. She arrived during the femoral stick.

"You will have to wait until Marilyn is hooked up to the machine," the dialysis nurse said. Erin Boggs waited outside with Tim, making small talk. After a few minutes, they were admitted. She sat down at my side.

"I am so glad you could come, Erin," I began.

"It took me awhile to get here. I am sorry," she said. "It must have been hard for you." Then the tubes to my left filled with blood. Her face suddenly drained of color and took on a green cast. "I'm sorry, Marilyn. I have to go." She stumbled out of M-2 to the bathroom. Tim and I looked at each other. "I guess this is not for everyone," he said ruefully.

Another day during the sandbag stage, I was lying prone and terrified to move when Dr. Rory Shore, a kidney specialist, strolled over.

"How are you, Marilyn?" he said, his delivery a clipped staccato.

"All right, I guess." I had no idea what to say. I wanted to say, "Can't you get me out of here?" Maybe he heard my cry on an inner level, because he replied, "Don't worry. You'll be on dialysis for awhile and then get a transplant."

I turned my head and refused to acknowledge him. I could not accept the fact of dialysis yet. I certainly was not ready for a transplant! I was so weak, so weary—barely this side of survival. I burrowed into my hospital bed, wanting to leave the whole mess behind me.

However, the fact remained that I would need a more permanent method of dialysis. Groin sticks could not continue forever, pleasant though they were! There could be blood clots in the legs used for access. Yet, for some reason, information seemed in short supply. It would seem that in a room full of dialysis patients, the answers would be forthcoming, but I was too shell-shocked to ask anyone. Residents and nurses suggested that I telephone dialysis centers and speak to the nurses there, so I called a Connecticut center. Their nurse was friendly and informative but I could hardly make sense of what she was saying. Even with my diminished reasoning capacity, I was beginning to see that asking a medical professional about dialysis was the wrong approach. It would be like asking a person who attends a symphony concert what it is like to play the violin.

Meanwhile, Dr. Christian, slipping into my room during afternoon rounds, was conducting his own research. After his examination, he encountered Tim in the hallway. "Could you bring Marilyn's violin from home?" he asked.

"Of course, Doctor."

Dr. Christian hurried away. I was curious. Why the strange request? The next day Tim brought the violin to my bed. The IV on my left arm restricted my movement, making it impossible to open the case. Tim opened it for me. We placed it on my neck just above my left shoulder and Dr. Christian observed exactly where it was held. To my amazement, he did not realize which side it was held on, or that the placements of a rubber tube on my neck would end my playing career. He was wondering if it was feasible to slice up an artery and insert a rubber tube for access, like the poor fellow I had observed at M-2! Although I could not play now, there was a remote possibility that I would have a career again. The doctor probably figured that my survival was at stake, reasoning that I would not have a career if I was dead. For my part, I felt that without music I might as well be dead. Fortunately, there were a few alternatives.

Tim and I discovered that there were two types of dialysis: hemodialysis and peritoneal. Hemodialysis involved the removal and cleansing of blood. Peritoneal involved the permanent insertion of a catheter into one's peritoneal cavity in the abdomen. Another access, besides the neck tube, for hemodialysis, involved the joining of a vein and an artery in the arm into a shunt or fistula. I was certain that this, also, would end my career. We asked Dr. Willy Steubenbord, my surgeon, about this method.

"There is a chance that a shunt in your arm could cause a twenty percent loss of sensation in the fingers," he said. The doctor was being cautious, but we were shocked. I could not play the violin without total control of my fingers in each hand. This method, also, would have to be discarded.

There seemed to be a gag order about dialysis information in the hospital. As beginners in the world of dialysis, we knew no one who could inform us, though any dialysis veteran would do. One evening, a resident from M-2 explained the two methods in a technical manner. We came away more perplexed than ever.

Finally, after frenzied deliberation, Tim and I chose the peritoneal method, deciding upon the lesser of two distasteful options. The consensus seemed to be that the peritoneal method was gentler and there were less fluid restrictions. A Continuous Cycle Peritoneal Dialysis machine could be obtained for us to use at home. Instead of the more common 24-hour method, termed CAPD, CCPD would require a relationship with a peritoneal machine for ten hours each night.

Three weeks minus a day after my hospital admission I had begun dialysis. After another week of dialysis every other day, the pounds had dropped off sufficiently that I could hoist my swollen legs over my bed of hell and take my first steps in three weeks. I felt like an elephant. Even with the walker, I was unused to the sensation of putting one leg in front of the other. Though still dazed from the poison in my system, I felt triumphant as I inched my way down the hall to the sunroom. I could sit in a chair now for a short period without pain. As the cars whizzed below on the F.D.R. Drive I sank into a tall chair and attempted to read.

I weighed 104. I had lost 60 pounds! It was easy to lose on the dialysis diet. I could not have potatoes or tomatoes and salt in any form, or embedded in any food. I was required to eat massive intakes of meat protein at every meal. This was a diet of unlimited sweets, extremely limited fluid intake and over-boiled vegetables. It was so abhorrent that eating became a distasteful chore, and I was usually nauseous.

There was one notable exception to this rule, however. After each dialysis session with its excruciating groin sticks, we had a choice of chicken or tuna salad sandwiches on white bread. I always chose tuna. This reward meant so much. After lying for four hours flat on my back, terrified of moving, with tubes connecting me to a machine that removed all of my blood, any respite was paradise. If I could not vacation on a beach in sunny Hawaii, a salty tuna sandwich would do.

Sessions were not always as carefree as described, however. Sometimes a machine would malfunction or my blood pressure would drop horrifyingly low. This felt like falling off the top of a skyscraper and waiting to hit bottom. I panicked and yelled for a doctor, hoping that he or she could remedy the imbalance before I died.

Occasionally I was to blame. At the beginning of the session I told the nurse how much fluid I wanted to take off and she would register the machine accordingly. We were weighed and the amount of fluid we had gained was calculated. Malfunctioning kidneys do not excrete fluid taken in. If the machine was programmed too aggressively, a disastrous dip in blood pressure was the result. Fortunately, this only happened a few times.

The doctors finally decided to sign my release papers. Four days shy of a month I had suffered in that abysmal room. It was the nadir of my existence. There was only one direction from here. Up.

Much as I would have liked to leave the hospital, doctors, dietitians, and even psychiatrists behind, this was not to be my fate. It was ironic. For fifteen years, I had rebelled against the Western health care system, feeling that the scientific, materialistic approach was limited in treating a chronic disease. Now the scientific community controlled my life in every respect. My only alternative was the harrowing death of kidney failure and I wasn't ready to choose that.

In the final few days of my stay, the doctors decided to insert a tankel catheter in my peritoneal cavity. Then, in approximately two weeks, I would switch from hemodialysis to peritoneal dialysis.

As I prepared to exit the room of hell, I was grateful to have survived. One morning I was sent up to the operating room, given the insertion operation, and then deposited in the kidney ward of the New York Hospital. I barely remember the process. I felt like a rag doll. I was ill-prepared to undergo another traumatic procedure, but the doctors had no choice. Oblivion was the best way to go through surgery anyway.

I awakened in a palatial room with the familiar violet-and-yellow-checked curtains. Tim's worried face stared down at me.

"Well, how was it?" he asked, grasping my hand.

"I don't know," I croaked, dismayed at the crusty sound I made. "They put a tube down my throat. It hurts." I forced a smile.

"I've been here for hours. I had no idea what was happening," Tim said. "You look okay, I guess."

My new roommate had also just returned from surgery. Her husband Mark sat by her bedside as they conversed in hushed tones. The surgeon had inserted a new shunt for hemodialysis on her left arm near the wrist. This shunt would join a vein and an artery so that the needles could be inserted in each to take the blood out of the body and then replace it, cleansed. Both arms retained numerous track marks and knotted areas where past shunts had been used and worn out. This new knot must have been painful. It was bleeding, but Ellen did not complain. Here, finally, was the dialysis veteran we sought. She and Mark operated their own hemodialysis machine in the basement of their home in New Jersey. Having been a dialysis patient for ten years, she was considerably patched up. It was amazing to me that she had survived at all. My brief experience had given me only a passing acquaintance with the superhuman struggles necessary to survive such a life. I felt a sense of awe at the person before me.

I asked about her profession. She told me that, when she was able, she took care of animals used in medical experiments. These animals had paved the way for procedures that saved my life. Though I had benefited from these experiments, I could not bear to think of the pitiful creatures tortured in the name of science. Ellen was a fighter. Her life seemed to consist of deprivations I would find impossible to endure; yet she accepted her lot and got on with it.

I stole glances at her, feeling an insatiable curiosity. Ellen challenged life to come up with tests for her indomitable spirit. I merely felt crushed by the weight of constant physical agony. I could not imagine a steady diet of this life of machine entrapment, fluid restriction, lack of water, omnipresent medical intrusion, and debilitating, crushing anemia. Tim and I wondered if Ellen and her husband represented the future that awaited us.

Ellen refused to consider a transplant. After ten years on dialysis, she feared that she would lose one of her sibling's kidneys to lupus. I could not decide if it was heroic or unfortunate that she felt so powerless against the disease. Yet, it was also possible that ten years on dialysis had depleted her to a point that could preclude acceptance of a new organ.

On January 6, 1989, weakened and skeletal, I was going home. It was a bittersweet parting. I would stay away from the New York Hospital for only a day at a time.

XVI.

Peritoneal Dialysis

My homecoming involved preparations for a life Tim and I found almost impossible to face. Inventories noted my fluid, salt, and vegetable and protein consumption while Tim learned to shop in the salt-free section of the supermarket. He prepared excellent dishes, laboring ceaselessly to tempt my reluctant palette. I was limited to three small glasses of water each day. This rationing gave me a real appreciation for the beauty of this basic fluid. Because I was often thirsty but could not drink, I sucked on candy to slake my thirst. It was a poor substitute for water, but it helped.

We received newsletters that warned us of the "dreaded potato" which attempted to create enthusiasm for the diet, but it was miserable privation. I had never liked meat and I hated chicken, which I seemed to have at every meal. Now at least four ounces of chicken or similar meat was required at both lunch and supper.

This diet was supposed to replace protein imbalances created by dialysis and nonfunctioning kidneys. I needed to eat in order to survive, and I was still functioning on the low end of survival. In a fatigued system, appetite is one of the first things to go. Appetite for food, sex, life.

Tim and I anxiously awaited the arrival of our CCPD machine while I continued the groin sticks in M-2 as an outpatient. Continuous cyclic peritoneal dialysis was supposedly a more humane way to dialyze. It involved taking a clear dialysate solution through the peritoneal catheter, allowing it to dwell in the peritoneal cavity for two hours, and then draining it out. Immediately afterwards another solution was inserted through the catheter and the procedure was repeated. Throughout the night four different cycles of fill, dwell and drain would accomplish the work of one healthy kidney, cleansing the blood of impurities. CAPD, the other, more common peritoneal dialysis method, involved a 24-hour fill and dwell and drain cycle. We decided against this method. I was hoping to resume my career on a limited basis, and I could not take breaks to change my bags.

Meanwhile we began a home training course in sterile technique. The peritoneal catheter lodged in a small hole to the left of my navel that had been surgically created. This tube wound through my peritoneal cavity and emerged outside of my stomach. A plastic cap that was to be carefully replaced after each dialysis covered it. Curled around inside my underwear, it felt like a huge tapeworm outside my body. The introduction of a single virus or bacteria into the tube could cause peritonitis, a potentially fatal infection. Baths, swimming or any other water contacts were forbidden. Showers would only be safe with a plastic bag over the sensitive cap. The fear of peritonitis was pervasive.

I sympathized with my dialyzing brothers and sisters, but sessions at the Rogosin Institute were a taxing nightmare. Fellow sufferers from all occupations passed through for survival treatments. I was still reeling from my hospital stay and could barely walk without assistance. This daze would not lift for some time. The dialysis machine enabled me to function at an absolutely minimal energy level.

My instructor, Angela, meant well. Her philosophy of tough love, stated with enthusiasm during my training, was to get on with your life while carrying massive quantities of fluid in your belly. In theory, this sounds possible. However, since Angela had not experienced this sensation physically, I felt a gap of understanding between us. We tend to categorize the people we work with. We teach students, serve clients and treat patients. The label often creates the distance. I surmised that her professional training even taught her to view me dispassionately.

Angela was a maternal woman, caring and warm. She made herself available to me night and day. Even so, I felt that she viewed me with a certain detachment. In our training sessions, she warned that crises of life-threatening proportion are easy to create when fluid is inserted in the belly through a plastic tube. She had obviously treated many in my condition. Yet, as I faced her every day, I wondered if she really saw me. To me it seemed that she did not make an effort to understand what I was experiencing.

As a professional musician, I can draw an analogy. When we play music, we bring the audience through the emotions our music evokes. In order to give a moving rendition of the notes on the page, if we are giving our best, we become the music. That is, we take on the prevalent mood of the piece. Health care professionals, to be most effective, should endeavor to maintain a self-protective distance while reserving a portion of them that could understand another's plight. This stance might hasten the healing process and narrow the gap between professional health care provider and vulnerable patient. In this way, the person in crisis becomes a fellow human being instead of a customer for services.

One lesson in particular stands out in my mind. We were to practice replacing the plastic cap on the tip of my rubber tube after the last bag drained out. I was so weak and disoriented that I did not have the strength to screw the little thing on. Fortunately, Tim was there. Collapsed with fatigue, I waited for Angela's appearance. I wondered why people treated me as if I was normal with stamina and understanding, when a huge chasm separated me from healthy people and they seemed to have no idea that it existed. Tim was the only one who knew. I described it to him as best I could.

After an anxious waiting period, the machine arrived. We had never held a life in our hands before, but, having completed the course, we began. The Herculean task of keeping me alive went to Tim. Meanwhile he accepted every playing engagement, begging contractors for work so that we would not sink deeper into debt.

Every evening after his concert Tim donned a surgical mask. Then he hung four ten-pound bags of dialysis fluid from a pole at the top of our CCPD machine. Each bag drained into my peritoneal cavity through the catheter in sequence. The fluid remained, or dwelled, there for two hours. Then it drained out into another bag at the bottom of the machine. The whole process took about ten hours from beginning to end. It was terrifying. To have pounds of fluid inserted quickly into my body felt like swallowing a watermelon whole. The bathroom was far from the machine, so I kept a bedpan near my bed. At first, we were thrilled with this method of dialysis. I would not be required to keep fluid in my belly twenty-four hours a day. However, we soon realized that I was chained to the machine through the tube I wore in my stomach for ten hours a night, nearly half of my life.

This plastic tapeworm defined my existence. The training films we saw during our course pictured it as an easier method, yet I was nauseous after every treatment. After Tim replaced my cap each morning, I threw up.

Our tiny bedroom became a surgical supply store. Peritoneal solution bags lined an entire wall. This reminded me of an acquaintance of my mother's in Richmond. He kept his bedroom wall stacked with an inexhaustible supply of Budweiser. Each night he drank beer after beer, watching television from his bed that faced this wall. His door locked from his children, he was a slave to his addiction, a hopeless alcoholic. I too was a slave. To survival.

We were to choose what strength of dialysate solution to use each night according to the fluid removed. Peritonitis was an ever-present risk. If the discarded fluid from my belly appeared cloudy, it might be peritonitis. Tim then injected antiseptic directly into my line. Afterwards he introduced a sample of the fluid into a test tube for analysis.

Because of the number of implements we needed, inventory was a necessity. We filled out requisition forms for hypodermic needles, surgical masks, rubber gloves and glass tubes. Each month we received a new delivery from the Baxter Company.

At our dialysis training session one day, a handsome young Baxter representative arrived to demonstrate the latest equipment. I wondered if he realized the lives his supplies saved, or knew the condition of their existence. I could not tell. Here was a dynamic, healthy businessman and we were his business. Somehow, an entrepreneurial approach to the dialysis life of bare survival seemed out of place. To me, the Baxter name represented the diminished state of my existence. It was a painful reminder of dialysis patients across the country that needed surgical implements to survive. I wondered if they shared my feelings about the pervasive medical technology foisted upon them. It was probably true that this gleaming state-of-the-art equipment would not exist without free-market competition. I was certainly grateful that I was the beneficiary of these advanced methods. In years past, I would have perished. Instead, I had become a bionic woman, dependent on technology to survive.

One day after we had completed a lesson at Rogosin, we went foraging for lunch in the neighborhood of the New York Hospital. We came upon a restaurant called Ottomanelli's. I was excited because I love to eat out. It was a celebration, almost like life before kidney failure. However, my heart sank when I saw the menu. There was nothing allowed on my diet! Salad was forbidden and each item on the menu contained salt. I realized that everything on my new diet was something I did not like. The prospect of slow starvation, or at least malnutrition, began to appear as a possibility.

Deprivation of water heightened my appreciation for it. I savored each rationed mouthful. The ability to urinate is also a discreet bodily function that most take for granted. I could still urinate, though many on dialysis cannot. In time, the function shuts down. My urine output was simply less efficient than it should have been.

My colleagues inquired if I was able to perform while on dialysis. They seemed to think that living on dialysis was a mild inconvenience. I had not played the violin since December 10, 1988. It was approaching February. Playing the violin was impossible for me while dialyzing. I could barely hold up my arms. Anemia affected my mental acuity. After dialysis treatments, I went to bed. My entire life now revolved around man's clumsy effort to replace what nature had so efficiently provided. The human kidney is roughly the size of a fist, yet machines that replace it stand approximately four feet tall. Either form of dialysis results in grievous bodily imbalances and anemia.

This necessity to tend to the body at all times and still feel horrid made the process seem hardly worth it. I began to think that death was better than the bare bones of existence I was living. I was accustomed to living my life as an expression of the soul, taking for granted the practical aspects of physical survival. My life had become an elementary school. Now I knew the meaning of the recurring dream about unlimited, unwanted schooling. Did this dream mean that I needed to learn my lessons and move on? I was not sure. The forest of my life was too thick to allow sunlight just yet.

I forced myself to practice, though it required an extraordinary effort to cut through the mental and physical haze. I missed making music. Fortunately, a Verdi Requiem performance began rehearsals on February 2nd and had a performance on February 4th. I eagerly accepted, willing myself to return to work. Weak and disoriented, I barely made it to the subway for the first rehearsal. Entering Carnegie Hall, I congratulated myself until I saw the short flight of stairs inside the entrance. It might as well have been Mount Everest. Hoping to appear inconspicuous, I slowly made my way up, grasping the railing. Paul Plishka, a singer from the Metropolitan Opera who was to be the bass soloist, was behind me. I was mortified that he had seen me in this condition.

The two-and-a-half hour rehearsals were a test of endurance. Though my stamina was gone, it was marvelous to participate in this great work. The brass section sounded like the loudest organ. The huge chorus and magnificent soloists were stunning. After the concert, I was proud of having returned to my profession. However, events to follow were to prove that my elation was premature.

The following day I attended a meeting of kidney patients. I respected their courage, but mingling with them was too painful. They seemed indicative of a future that awaited me. I felt no camaraderie, just bone-numbing exhaustion. My horror at this prospect made me want to be anywhere else. I was new to the dialysis way of life. For me, the onslaught of constant medical intrusion was overwhelming, yet I sensed that these dialysis patients accepted their set of conditions without question. With no energy to socialize, I felt more depressed than ever. I returned to my machine disconsolate.

On Monday morning, February 6th, I was thankful to have survived the interminable ten hours of fill, dwell and drain. Tim had just emptied the drainings into the toilet when he heard a small voice from the bedroom.

"I'm not feeling well, honey." He dropped his tray and rushed to my side.

"Would you like some cereal?" Tim frowned. "Let me take your temperature." He inserted the thermometer into my mouth and left the room. Suddenly he heard a crash. Hastening back to the bedroom, he found me on the floor. I had bitten the thermometer in half. The pupils of my eyes had rolled up into my head. Foam drooled from the corners of my mouth. Tim slipped the blood pressure cuff on my gyrating arm. The reading was over 200. Panicking, he was terrified to leave me for a second. He summoned Dr. Collins, a cardiologist whose office was located across the hall. The doctor ran to my room where I was still gyrating on the floor.

"Did she swallow the glass?" Tim asked.

"No, I don't think so. But she's having grand mal seizures." Dr. Collins placed a nitroglycerin patch on my chest, but I continued to have one seizure after another. He called an ambulance. During the forty-five minutes it took for them to arrive, I experienced several more grand mal seizures in succession.

Finally, the paramedics entered the bedroom with a stretcher and wheeled my shaking body through the hallway to the street.

"Could you take us to New York Hospital, please?" Tim hoped he sounded calm.

"Our ambulance goes to St. Luke's," the driver stated flatly, closing the ambulance door.

"That's not acceptable. Marilyn's records and doctors are at New York Hospital!" Tim yelled. The driver shook his head, but pointed the vehicle in the right direction.

As the ambulance crawled through rush hour traffic, with no siren or flashing lights, Tim asked, "Can't you go faster?" Minute after agonizing minute passed as the vehicle inched its way across town. Tim was certain I would be dead by the time they reached the hospital. They were punishing us for Tim's insistence on the New York Hospital.

Throughout the ordeal, fortunately, I do not remember a thing. I was conscious just before my first seizure and subsequently left my body for three days. This out-of-body astral journey was a welcome respite from affairs as they were. During my travels, I experienced no pain. No fill and dwell cycles. No anemia. My soul roamed free and clear, unshackled by the machine. Finally, I awakened in a gray, windowless room. My father's concerned face peered down at me. I smiled. Was I dreaming? My body felt like a rock thudding to earth as significant parts of me continued to float above the room.

Slowly, gently, I reoriented myself to the physical. Tim had spent an agonizing three days wondering if I would survive. He informed me that my arrival at the hospital had brought an instantaneous gathering of doctors. Even with this flurry of skilled attention, I had almost died. Tim had paced the hospital corridors, incapacitated by this latest crisis. Though he had quit smoking, he started again. Mastering sterile technique had been tough, he thought, but he could handle that. It was the feeling of helplessness he hated. Now his wife was near death again. It was another crisis in an unending line.

Tim had shouldered more than his share of responsibility throughout his life. Now that his wife was an invalid, it was fortunate that he possessed great stamina. His loving care had expanded our love beyond limits. Invisible cords of love as real as my umbilical catheter connected us.

After I became coherent again, the doctors prescribed seizure medication, resulting in what I can only call my zombie phase. Phenobarbital and dylantin are powerful inhibiting drugs. Phenobarbital slows the brain. Unfortunately, my life came to a stop as well. Performances were impossible, but at least most of the time I was blissfully unconscious.

Tim labored valiantly on the machine every night. So far, I had avoided the contraction of peritonitis so we had achieved dialysis success. He continued to feed me the unappetizing renal diet and I continued to throw it up. I often wondered if dialysis success meant survival. I could not figure what the other benefits were.

Winter faded into spring. In spite of Tim's efforts, life for me was an abysmal chore. In the early afternoon, I glimpsed a splash of amber sunlight over the red brick building across the street. It was the highlight of my day. My best friends called frequently. Many of my colleagues whom I had believed to be friends, shocked at my gaunt appearance, fell away. They did not know what to say to me. I didn't care. Most of the time I was oblivious, anyway. My semiconscious state was like a thermal blanket insulating me from the world.

Each night began with the dwell cycle, the fluid remaining in my belly for two hours. After it was drained the entire process was repeated three more times each night. To distract me from the agony of the first fill cycle Tim often tempted my reluctant palate with sherbet. My peritoneal cavity rebelled at the sudden expansion. I had to fight the impulse to throw up or grasp the tube and pull it out of my body. The pain of the first pump and dwell cycle made sleep impossible. The necessity to remain still for ten hours, instead of the four of hemodialysis, slowly became more painful. Theoretically, I could walk while on the machine, but this was so uncomfortable that I gave up trying. There were no vacations from my nightly ten-hour shackle, no escape from my situation. It was indeed difficult to explain that my machine was my most intimate companion.

By May, I was able to return to work playing concerts as we had hoped. I would now become a musician by day and an invalid at night. I downplayed my condition, determined that my colleagues should not know the schizophrenic nature of my existence. Tim and I played with the American Symphony in a screening of the silent film epic *Napoleon*, scored and conducted by Carmine Coppola. The film lasted three-and-a-half hours at the Radio City Music Hall. The pit was raised during our performance. There was no exit until it was over. Many musicians complained about having to hold their bladders for three-and-a-half hours. I did not have that problem. My machine performed that service. Again I felt set apart, entrapped in a cage of dependency.

During our brief intermissions, Tim made certain that I ate a tuna sandwich and took my blood pressure pills. My musician friends, who were leading normal lives, did not understand the immediacy of attending to my medical needs. Tim found it difficult to accept that our colleagues did not know what we were going through. He felt that we were adrift in an ocean of indifference. However, I realized that they had no frame of reference for our experience. As individual beings, we live from the inside out. Our inner world gives us the motivation to feel. Compassion changes our focus, but many do not recognize another's need unless prompted. I was comfortable with this distance. It kept my insulation intact.

In spite of my temporary employment, I felt like a failure. It was June and I had been on dialysis for six-and-a-half months. My life was so limited. Disability payments were not available to me as a free-lance musician without a regular job. When I discussed my feelings with the social worker at Rogosin, she referred me to a government social worker. Donning a maroon dress with an ambiguous waistline that concealed my plastic appendage, I traveled to Mrs. Haddings' cubbyhole, which overlooked a dingy courtyard near Penn Station. One corner accommodated a three-foot-high stack of cases just like me.

"So you're a musician! I love music! My husband and I attend the opera regularly. My son plays the trumpet. You must love it! The violin is my favorite instrument," she gushed.

"I do love it, Mrs. Haddings. However, it is not going so well just now. Most of the time I am in bed. I don't have the energy to play any more."

She looked at me and sighed. "Life does continue, dear. You have been through so much. Why don't you see this man? He will test you for something a little less taxing." She handed me a business card.

I made an appointment and, a few days later, traveled to Mr. Radkin's office in the same area of midtown. He led me through a dingy hallway into a small room separated by a dirty glass partition. The psychiatrist acted as if there was a secret he was keeping from me. After a demeaning battery of simple tests, he pronounced that I was depressed. I was surprised at this diagnosis. Other than occasional mood swings, I had never been depressed before. However, recent events had destroyed my equilibrium. I had to admit that the future looked bleak.

Next, I took aptitude tests. After the results were evaluated, I began to consider computer programming. Wimberly, a former cellist who had received a successful transplant, sparked my interest. Wimberly became a mentor to me. She was unable to play her cello through the years of kidney failure. After the transplant Wimberly quit the cello and made a new life for herself. She learned to be a programmer, got a job at IBM and bought a house in New Jersey. Wimberly and her husband had made successes of their lives.

Weighing the alternatives, I decided to become a programmer on the strength of her example. Supposedly, musicians make good programmers. They are thorough and accustomed to solving problems as well as working alone in a practice room. Math had not been my favorite subject in school. The new arbiters in my life now decided that I needed remedial math instruction.

I attended a math class in the Penn Station area. After the subway ride, I attempted to elude the sea of commuters that almost knocked me down. I climbed a flight of stairs and found a dirty, cramped space where a noncommittal woman asked me to fill out a few papers. Then I went to a small classroom that seated five people. Two of my classmates were lame and one had a learning disability. Our lethargic teacher sat at her desk yawning and doing her nails. Again, I felt invisible. The workbooks were on a third-grade level, yet I could not seem to focus. The partitioned room without windows was stifling, the expectation of our teacher low. The students attempting to improve their lives were treated with condescension. I had never viewed the world as a handicapped person before. Now I felt a kinship with these people who had slipped through the cracks of the welfare system.

My life was slipping further out of control. I had lost the will to live. There was no energy to pursue my career. It was time to reassess before I became lost in an abyss of social programs and regimented medical care. I had created this downward spiral, and I was the only one who could change its direction.

XVII.

Spiritual Healing

Dismayed at the diagnosis of depression, I intensified my spiritual search. My prospects for the future looked bleak. If I relied on my machine, I would become an invalid. Yet, if I healed myself through faith, I might have a chance to take back my life. As Jesus said, "Ask, and ye shall receive. Knock, and it shall be opened unto you."

Throughout each wrenching crisis, I had implored the God of mercy to see me through to survival. The twenty-third Psalm had helped me through the darkest nights of kidney failure. I was desperate to believe that if the Higher Intelligence could allow such dramatic falls from grace, it surely could accomplish a healing.

Two years earlier when it seemed obvious that my kidneys might fail, I had called a psychic healer who had written a renowned book on the subject of spiritual healing.

"Brenda," I began. "I was so inspired by your book. It shows us that there is so much more to the process of illness than the medical establishment acknowledges."

"I'm glad you think so," she said.

"As a matter of fact, my kidneys are failing. I need help and I was hoping you might be able to see me."

"I don't see patients personally any longer. However, I am teaching a seminar in Bali in a few weeks. Would you like to come?"

"Uh, no thanks. But thanks for your time." She seemed not to have heard me. How could she turn away someone in need? However, after I gave it some thought I realized that, unlike my previous 'healer', she was not a charlatan. She did not promise health and instead make me worse. My kidney failure, years in the making, was not going to vanish in an instant, much as I wished that it were so. It would be necessary to look inward for the answers.

In studying the inner causes of my condition I returned to Louise Hay's *You Can Heal Your Life*. Her book made total sense to me. Her affirmations always made me feel better and connected me to a larger whole. In following the book's plan for action I realized that it would be necessary to search out the imbalances which had led me to turn my body against itself.

Accordingly, I reevaluated the process of guilt. Guilt is remorse for not having made other choices in dealing with one's problems. It is a static and backward-looking emotion for impetuous people. I regretted instances of misbehavior and selfish actions—events where I acted first and thought about it later. Usually the only person I hurt was me, but this was not always the case.

Ms. Hay proclaimed that kidney patients felt themselves to be failures and simply gave up. I was frustrated that I had not achieved more stability in my career. Yet I had worked so hard to become a violinist. If I was to effect a cure, I would need to remove years of habitual thought patterns which created an unhealthy need for these situations of punishment and suffering. Neither lupus nor kidney failure victims felt they were worthy of healthy, productive lives.

I believe that lupus asserts itself as a method for relinquishing control over one's life. An unspoken message in my household as I was growing up was that women are secondary. A dependency pattern emerged when my marriage failed as I had allowed David's career to take precedence. Though consciously happy with my decision to serve him as less than an equal partner, I was ignoring many inner needs. I could never feel complete as an adornment for a man. I wanted to earn my own prestige. After David and I parted, I explored my potential alone. This was important in assessing my career and personal motives.

Tim and I have always been equal partners. However, I often retained a stubborn willfulness with which I fought Dr. Christian on many occasions. When lupus struck I gave up and let Tim take care of me. I had observed a similar relationship between my parents. Both my mother and myself, feeling safe in a stable relationship, effected a subconscious surrender to the life of dependence made possible in marriage.

Now I realized that, however much Tim helped me, only independence would save me. I had been to the golden tunnel before I married Tim. There I had learned that death is not a fearful event. In fact, I longed to return to that perfect world of love and acceptance. When life-threatening manifestations of lupus pulled me away from the earth plane, I was glad to ride the balloon to the stratosphere. Although I found these finer dimensions preferable to life on earth, Tim pulled me back repeatedly until I finally realized the value of my opportunity for growth here.

I had attempted a faith healing through Christian Science and failed, but I still believed it was possible. Even after all my experiences, I stubbornly refused to embrace the disease as 'mine'. I felt certain that it was an abnormal state, an illusion. This thinking goes against medical knowledge, yet I knew at the very base of my being that my theory was true.

I relived my childhood in search of clues. In my early years, Mother had been independent and fun loving. Then at some level she must have buried her dreams, sacrificing a promising career to raise a family. I often sensed she was living vicariously through me. When her hands, which had once charmed her devoted audiences on the piano and organ, became twisted with arthritis and imprisoned in braces, it must have been heartbreaking to give up her first love, music.

The lupus and rheumatoid arthritis that caused her gradual deterioration brought our family to its knees. As my mother gave up in small increments, everyone around her—her husband, mother, sister and doctors supported her abdication. I could not understand it. Why not encourage her to beat the disease? Lupus had wrestled her to the ground. I was not going to allow this to happen to me.

When she died, the nucleus of our family was gone. We have never recovered from the damage left in its wake. I hated lupus. It was like a hurricane. I was glad that my mother never saw my kidneys fail. I had suffered enough with her. I did not want her to suffer with me. It was not hard to understand why I rebelled against my fate of abnormality, fighting the beliefs that this condition was real. Obviously, I had manifested lupus and kidney failure with certain predictable results. However, there was much more involved than this physical reality. In every instance, before a flare, there had been months or years of certain patterns of thought, which were mental responses to conditions in my life. A wrathful God did not punish me. I had punished myself.

Fortunately, each time I had gotten myself into a crisis, the doctors had saved me. Moreover, I had caused more suffering for myself by my willful refusal to accept the medical label defining my particular symptom until it was too late. I was an exasperating patient. Unlike my mother, I wanted to know everything possible about my treatment. More than once I had caused Dr. Christian to throw up his hands. Yet, my rebellion could be a positive force. Our doctor-patient relationship was not set up as a dialogue, but I had insisted upon it. Now it was imperative that I intelligently marshal this fighting spirit with all the strength at my disposal.

Entering meditative states at every opportunity, I unearthed wrongs from my childhood, early traumas, and disappointments over my career, anger at doctors who had hurt me, and any other negative emotion I could dig up. It was a considerable task. Habits of a lifetime are not easily erased. Fortunately, I possessed unlimited time for this spiritual work.

Saddened though I was that I had lupus, and, even worse, kidney failure, I was beginning to see how I had created an opportunity for these conditions to flourish. A self-defeating dependency syndrome had developed within me. Consciously I did not desire to be an invalid. I loved to work and hated placing our financial obligations on Tim. The disease seemed to come when I least expected it, but my subconscious had created these situations.

I now set about the daunting task of satisfying these dependency needs in healthier ways. First, however, it would be necessary to free myself from the dialysis machine and a life of dependency. Conventional prayer had never felt natural to me. Asking an omniscient power to help me in my petty little needs had always seemed unbelievably presumptuous. Now my life was at stake. For this, I could summon plenty of emotion. For my healing to be successful, I would need a pure and burning desire, even an obsession, that I would be healed. To accomplish this it would be necessary to suspend previous beliefs and operate on pure faith. Thus, countless times, I set about imagining myself healthy and free. Stripping myself of every learned concept, I got down on my knees and bared my soul to my Creator. I became, to the best of my ability, my pure self, my own highest soul.

With great emotion, force and expectation I requested health. Ignoring statistics of the impossibility of my demand, I proceeded to ask God for help. I became new. I hinged everything on the outcome, yet I expected nothing.

Slowly my creatinine and BUN (measures of toxins in the blood, or the kidney's efficiency in clearing them) began to normalize. Dr. Sullivan became more elated with each visit. On one unforgettable day, he walked into the CAPD room beaming.

"These numbers are incredible! I could count the kidney patients who have been healed on one hand!" he exclaimed. "With this proof that your kidneys are working again, we'll be able to take you off the machine! How is this possible?"

There was a flurry of activity as the other CAPD patients gathered around me, wide-eyed.

"What happened? Did you eat a special diet? How did you do it?'

"It was faith, just faith, my sisters."

"Well, praise the Lord."

"Yes. Praise the Lord."

XVIII.

Remission

After being on the dialysis machine for nine-and-a-half months, I was in remission. The machine was taken away; the boxes, needles and masks no longer needed. My modest bedroom restored, I resumed my career as a violinist.

It was October 12, 1989, the day my catheter would be removed. I was scheduled to rehearse with an orchestra. This particular afternoon was also the only available appointment time with my busy surgeon. I would be free again! I could not wait to take my plastic lifeline out. Though it had saved my life, it was frightening to live with this appendage. The thought of my freedom filled me with joy. I could hardly believe it was actually happening. Surely the contractor who had hired me could understand the magnitude of it, and that I would have to be excused from the rehearsal. I was mistaken. I was dismissed from the concert and I would never play in this group again.

I had neglected to describe my odyssey through kidney failure and dialysis to this man. Possibly, if I had done so, he may have been more sympathetic. My colleagues would never know that I had been on the brink of losing everything from my life to my career and had come back through will, courage and the help of God. I could accept the small disappointments. I was free! I drank in a new gratitude forged from the magnitude of this miracle. I was so grateful to play the violin again. I had played sporadically since becoming an invalid on dialysis, always with half of my usual energy and concentration. Hard as I tried to appear normal, I was barely functioning.

I was thrilled to be back with the Opera Orchestra of New York as a normal person again—not hooked up to a machine for ten hours a night or having my blood removed three times a week. During my time on dialysis, I had observed the privileged and talented musicians on the stage of Carnegie Hall without knowing if I would ever be able to rejoin them. From this vantage point I realized the magic of music making and the special joy it brought others.

A musician must have the concentration of a surgeon to execute the technical demands placed upon her. Training involves years of practice from an early age, followed by intensive study in college and graduate school. It is a life of total dedication and exacting skill as each artist works to become a pure channel for the great masterworks to manifest themselves. I became a musician for this reason. In addition, a musician must have great physical endurance. Jobs are scarce and competition is fierce. For every orchestra or Broadway position, there are hundreds of amply qualified candidates. These are highly educated and skilled musicians, especially the younger ones, who have had the benefit of advanced training techniques.

Earlier, before this miraculous remission, I had become uncertain that I still possessed the physical endurance to continue in this demanding profession. After my tests with the social workers and psychologists were completed, I enrolled in a computer-programming course at Baruch College. Though I tried to muster enthusiasm for programming, I just did not get it. The Cobol concepts whizzed somewhere over my head. The artistic temperament that I had nurtured all my life was incompatible with this analytical practice. I enjoyed the computer, but the interior workings would benefit more from those who enjoyed systems work. My lack of understanding now reinforced my sense of failure. Programming was an alternative I chose because I had lost the stamina to play the violin. Nevertheless, I always hoped I would return. Playing the violin was my destiny and most difficult challenge.

When my doctors discovered that I was a violinist, they often quizzed me about the life of a performer. I found that many doctors had studied the violin or a stringed instrument, often leaving their studies for the security of medicine. Having tasted the sweet melodies that funnel through us, they were aware of a void in themselves. In answer to their queries, I would describe favorite pieces and performances. They seemed to enjoy my descriptions. Through this process, in the isolation of the hospital without my beloved music to play, I also realized how much I needed it for the survival of my soul.

My programming instructor also loved violin music. At a party celebrating the end of our class, as we discussed the Mendelssohn Concerto, my heart yearned to be playing it. Talking about playing an instrument is like being a spectator. It is not my style. I want to participate. This conversation reinforced my sense that I was in the wrong place.

So, stamina or not, I returned to playing wholeheartedly. Unfortunately, the pressure of performance forced my blood pressure up, which further damaged my kidneys. Dr. Sullivan urged me to maintain the delicate balance I had so recently restored, but this admonition would have me sitting at home in placid, motionless survival. I could have taken the programming diploma and turned down my playing work, but I decided instead to leave programming. I was a violinist. This is what I had trained my entire life to do. I knew that there was a risk involved in continuing playing which involves pressure and stress. Certain concerts contained more pressure than others did. If I were playing solo or chamber music, where the every note is 'exposed', there would obviously be more pressure to produce than if I was playing in a violin section.

My kidneys had sustained damage from the initial attack, and this included an unfortunate rise in blood pressure. Performing might exacerbate this. Nevertheless, I needed performing to survive. During my darkest days of dependence on the dialysis machine, I felt destitute because we all need food for our souls. As a musician, I supply that food, stealing nourishment for myself in the process.

I soared again with the musical masters, desperately needing to put mundane medical concerns behind me. Unfortunately, I was careless in monitoring my blood pressure. Eight-and-a-half months of blissful health had passed when tests revealed that my creatinine and BUN were rising again. I entered the Hospital for Special Surgery for another pulse therapy. The prospect of repeating dialysis filled me with fear. I raged over my carelessness.

In July Dr. Sullivan faced me squarely.

"Marilyn, your BUN is 10, your creatinine 80.1. You'll have to go back on dialysis."

"What? No, it can't be!" A knot of fear formed in my stomach. I was furious. It was Dr. Sullivan's fault. He could not make me return to dialysis. I would not stand for it.

"I'm sorry, but that's the way it is. I do not want you to suffer from renal poison. We should put you back on the machine soon."

"I won't do it!" I spat out.

"You'll have to, Marilyn." He was kind, but he was also firm. I hated him. This was cruel punishment. In my haste to resume a normal life, I had not given enough attention to my spiritual transformation. The healing would remain only as long as I stayed at higher levels. Searching my soul with brutal honesty, I had to admit that I was to blame instead of Dr. Sullivan, who was concerned that I would not decline further.

I lapsed into self-pity and denial. Hoping to postpone the inevitable, I asked Dr. Sullivan for permission to travel to Saratoga with Tim who was playing the New York City Ballet summer season, and he agreed to a grace period.

We took our cats Mare and Bubby, Max's replacement, to Saratoga and settled deep in the woods. It was quiet and restful. The previous year a chance encounter in Saratoga was to have repercussions for years to come. At that time a special CCPD machine was delivered and assembled especially for us. During this miserable summer, I had no energy to do anything except read, so I devoured every spiritual book I could find. I attempted to play tennis by myself and once walked into town, but these efforts totally exhausted me. One day Tim happened upon a newspaper ad for a psychic fair in Albany. On a beautiful Sunday, we drove there. A behemoth maze of state buildings confronted us. It looked like a Martian city. Finally, we spotted a sign for the fair. We almost floated down the hall, as if pulled by some strange gravitational force. A large woman with flowing red hair was in the center of the fluorescent-lighted room, sitting at a desk with a plumed feather. It was as if the entire room revolved around her. She had solidity, a presence built of otherworldly strength.

I wondered if she sensed that I was at the lowest ebb of my life and that I had been soaking up spiritual solutions. When she invited us to her home, I realized that she sensed this and more. Mary had taken us on absolute faith based upon one meeting. We were sustained by her trust.

Her home was small and in need of paint, but inside a meeting of advanced metaphysicians was taking place. A well-known author, Warren Gill, attended, along with two couples from Albany and New York. They seemed to view us from another dimension. Her husband and two engaging girls crowded into the small living room. A menagerie of cats and dogs tussled underfoot.

I was awed to be in Mr. Gill's presence. I wanted to ask him many questions, but he began by asking me one.

"What do you know of the Tree of Life?" he asked.

"Well, nothing, really," I replied.

"Then we have nothing to discuss." He waved me away.

Despite this dismissal, I remained fascinated. What was this mysterious "Tree of Life" and why did my lack of knowledge preclude our discussion? I shelved this information away for future use.

Mary advised me against following a noted guru who advised chanting, and gave me the titles of several books by Mr. Gill. After our visit, I worked on these concepts and they contributed greatly to my healing.

Now, one year later, we had reached another crisis. We called and made an appointment to see her again. Her house was still in need of paint, but when we stepped into her living room, it was like an oasis. Again, her presence was extraordinary. I moved toward her, seeking the light she seemed to emanate.

"You've healed yourself. Congratulations." She sat in the corner on a large easy chair. A floral dress covered her ample figure. Her light Irish skin seemed to glow in the dim room. "But, in order to maintain it, you need a lot of energy. This energy would enhance other areas of your life. Your music, for instance." She smiled.

"What about my computer studies, Mary?"

"Let them go. Continue with music," she said. "This is where your true self lies. And get a transplant. It will change your life."

"But I am concerned about the drugs I'll have to take."

"Let me suggest certain herbs which will minimize the stimulating effect of prednisone. These should restore your balance."

Sustained with a new sense of purpose, we thanked her and took our leave to face the challenges of the future. During the last few days in Saratoga, I began to realize what the future would entail. One night I ate a ham sandwich, cheating on my low-salt diet. My blood pressure rose to a dangerous level. The next morning I lost my cereal all over the front lawn. Later I walked several blocks to the pool and swam thirty laps on willpower alone. I barely staggered home through the sweltering heat. During the ride back to New York, I was wretched, certain that I needed help.

On Monday, July 23, 1990, the femoral stick was inserted into my groin in the M-2 pavilion again. Throughout my stay in Saratoga I had grappled with denial, raging at the inattention which had allowed me to slip back into the helpless reality of dialysis. Though the familiar sense of failure returned, this condition mandated that I find a place of acceptance. My fighting spirit emerged.

Though I had arrived at the brink of invalidism and barely escaped it many times, I could not face dialysis again. I would perish on the system. In the past, I had escaped irreversible injury because of luck and a certain instinct for self-preservation. Now it became apparent that if I must face dialysis again, I must seek a transplant at the earliest opportunity. There is a deterioration inherent in dialysis. This unforgiving process often brings about grievous imbalances. Because of the unhealthy diet as well as the process of replacing blood, I often observed that veterans were thin, seriously anemic, and eventually became invalids. Extended use of either dialysis method was weakening and ultimately fatal. Many may argue that patients survive on dialysis for many years. I admire these people because for me this would be very difficult.

My best chance for success was a living, related donor with the most tissue matches.

Now the painful task of calling my relatives faced me. My younger brother Jeffrey, an unmarried respiratory therapist, volunteered and sent tissue-matching blood work from his place of employment, the Medical College of Virginia.

Because I was unable to get to and from dialysis without help, my father had volunteered to stay with me. One day, at an appointment for a transplant orientation session at the New York Hospital, Dad charmed the medical staff with his humor and impressed them with his youthful demeanor. After the session was over a nurse asked, "Would you consider being a donor?"

"But I'm 71 years old!" he protested.

"That's amazing. You certainly don't look it. Let us test you, and anything out of the ordinary will take you out of consideration."

"I'm game, I guess," he smiled uncertainly.

We discovered that my father had a better tissue match than my brother! This would increase my chances of acceptance. Dad was called into duty again, this time for the biggest sacrifice of his life. If he felt ambivalent, he never let me know. He had watched his wife taken from him in increments. Now, having witnessed his daughter slide from crisis to crisis, he was glad to take an active role in returning her to a normal life. Excitedly we prepared for the transplant.

XIX.

Dialysis Revisited

Now a dialysis veteran, I was expected to reacquaint myself with the femoral stick routine. I was glad that my peritoneal catheter was gone, although renal failure had reoccurred. I had richly enjoyed my time of freedom. Unfortunately, it would be necessary to select a method of permanent access again. Spending half my life chained to a machine with a tube in my stomach was an experience I did not want to repeat. Hemodialysis, though brutal and painful, took only a few hours three times a week. Tim and I decided to take a chance on a fistula, which is the joining of a vein and an artery. We would use my upper right arm, the arm that draws the violin bow, and hope for the best.

We scheduled a surgery date with Dr. Willy Steubenbord. In the meantime, I returned to the M-2 ward as an outpatient. As I searched my soul for acceptance of my situation, I decided that the only way I could face dialysis again was to expect nothing. I shut down and minimized my desires and dreams. I would be grateful for a modicum of happiness but I would not seek it out. I intensified my spiritual studies, which became my purpose for survival.

There was a large wooden bench down the hall from M-2. Tim always brought me in time for my treatment but the machine was never ready. While awaiting the call for the dreaded first stick I focused on my breathing and became serene, working to attain right mind, as the Buddhists call it.

I was grateful to the nurses who operated the machines, working tirelessly to help me survive. During the four hours I lay motionless I would inquire after their families. One nurse, a beautiful woman with blonde hair named Adele, showed me pictures from her daughter's wedding in the Caribbean. Another, my favorite, was a Filipino woman who had been with me from the beginning. Only five feet tall and weighing around ninety pounds, she was a tiny dynamo who worked tirelessly to keep the dialysis patients in M-2 alive. We often chatted during dialysis. During our talks, she revealed a few details about her life. She lived alone and often worked brutal, consecutive shifts. For a brief moment, I shared her normal, healthy life. It made a handy substitute for my own, again waiting in the wings. And afterwards, there were those luscious tuna sandwiches!

Every other day Tim drove me across town to M-2. After I was dialyzed, I felt so devastated I could barely walk. Dizzy with exhaustion and shock, I was driven home and spent the rest of the day in bed. The next day I was still recovering. There was no energy for a normal life.

Tim and I were still nervous about the shunt operation joining a vein and an artery just above my right elbow, because the slightest loss of sensation in my right arm would put a stop to my career. Fortunately, the procedure was a stunning success, thanks to the artistry of Dr. Steubenbord. There was no damage to my bow arm. My new shunt, a raised area the size of a rope, extended for three inches just above and inside my right elbow. The nurses encouraged me to pump it up in order that their needles would 'take' directly on the first stick. I sometimes placed my ear over the joined vein and artery. There I could hear a loud, rhythmic gushing of blood. It was an eerie sensation. It seemed my arm could hardly contain the force of it.

After a two-week recovery period, my new shunt was ready. I would dialyze in the Helmsley Pavilion, the Rogosin kidney center, instead of

M-2. At this time, there was some bad publicity about Leona Helmsley. I felt she had been misrepresented. She gave generously for the opulent facility that saved the lives of many people, including my own.

Two needles were stuck into my arm—one for the vein and one for the artery. I sat in a reclining chair instead of a stretcher and watched the other dialysis patients come and go. At my first treatment, the nurse stuck my new shunt repeatedly. These sessions were more frightening than the femoral sticks, not only because of the pain but also because I could see what was happening to my precious bow arm.

The switch to Helmsley was a shock. Here, finally, were the long-term dialysis veterans we had sought years ago. Most of them were painfully thin; their arms lacerated with needle marks and raised shunts new and old. As I became weaker and developed a yellow-brown caste to my skin, I joined legions of dialysis patients whose appearance was a natural result of the restrictive diet that siphoned weight off. My colleagues even complimented me on my thin appearance. There is an emphasis on thinness in our society, especially for women. I had achieved thinness, but it was a Pyrrhic victory. Giving up my life in exchange for a little fat was not the tradeoff I had in mind.

Many of my dialysis comrades walked with crutches, the result of failed transplants. Some attended school and others held down jobs. They seemed to have normal lives. I was not a member of this heroic group. After the shunt healed, I could perform only in a limited capacity. Most of the time I remained prone and totally exhausted.

Again I was chained to a dialysis machine, but now I had the luxury of an entire day between treatments during the week and two on weekends. This was something I had missed on peritoneal dialysis. During my days of freedom, I was not a dialysis patient—I was a normal human being. Only when I arrived at the New York Hospital would I admit the reality of it. Without this selective amnesia, I could not face it. My new permanent hemodialysis process took all of my blood and returned it, cleansed. Somehow, a part of me was misplaced in the process. It took an entire day to get over this crushing feeling.

It was the kind of summer which melted my soul, and I was an invalid again. Tim was offered the first flute position in the Chautauqua Orchestra, a nine-hour drive away. He could not turn it down. We needed every penny. My mother-in-law and father agreed to look after me while he was away. Each would stay with me for a few weeks to 'shunt' me back and forth to dialysis. I expected that there would be no gains other than to grit my teeth and skim the surface of bare subsistence. I found, to my surprise, that it was a valuable summer in many ways. I would confront some important issues in my life. New York never felt like home, even after almost twenty years. I wanted to leave, to find a nice, quiet place to burrow. But how would we ever dig ourselves out of our mountain of debt? After kidney failure, the Catastrophic Illness Act had enabled me to join Medicare. This made our medical bills much more reasonable. However, we were still deep in debt for the previous hospitalizations and doctor fees that our insurance did not cover.

Again, I had sunk to the nadir of my existence. Here I looked for nothing. I became nothing. I wanted nothing. My hopes and dreams were dead and I would not entertain them. There was nowhere to run, nowhere to hide. No vacation from dialysis. I was stuck on the bottom of a stack of city dwellers. I had lost everything I loved, so I shut down and reduced my life to minimal survival, focusing on the tiny pilot light that remained. Consumed with spiritual work, I absorbed everything written which could guide me to a greater understanding.

After a suitable period of grieving, I decided to make the best of things. I cleaned out accumulated paperwork in Tim's area of the apartment. I took long walks in Riverside Park with my friends, alone, and with my parents, and imagined a place of safety where I would not be on public display in my time of weakness. This place would be a protected, beautiful environment that would satisfy all of my needs. It would be far away from the loud and stressful city. With this in mind, I began to construct a future drawn to my specifications.

For many years, I had internalized the attitudes around me. At rehearsals and concerts, I agreed with my colleagues' complaints. I thought a musician's life was supposed to be miserable. Now, from the outside looking in, I reassessed the process of attitude. Playing music for a living is a privilege, not a pain. I decided that henceforth I would savor every rehearsal and concert with gratitude. Sadly, much of the time I lacked enough energy to play the violin. Therefore, instead, I confronted the bare bones of life without illusion.

I faced my life in earnest, all the while making mental plans to pull myself up and away. After each dialysis, I stated Louise Hay's affirmations. The theory behind these affirmations is to put good energy in front of bad. By saying the positive statements I could replace my life with fantasy, the life I preferred to have instead of the one I was living. Being grateful for every blessing that I could find, I began to bring more good into my life. Rather than squelching the flow of bounty by thoughts of depression, I looked for the most positive elements in every situation. It was not easy. My existence was so elemental that the hopeful aspects were glistening flecks among the sand. Though I searched to find a positive thread and hold fast to it, usually the heat, grime, and crushing weight of anemia beat me down.

During the weekend, I did my best to forget dialysis. Then the process started all over again. It was impossible not to decline quickly in this situation. I realized the imperative to escape the process. It would not take long for my health to spiral downward past hope of repair.

An expanding list of doctors catered to my declining health. When my eyes became inflamed, we learned that I had burst a blood vessel from high blood pressure. It was difficult to patch up this or that problem while the brutal, consuming process of blood removal and replacement continued. Too much was lost. This cycle would escalate as my health quickly deteriorated.

One day I got a call from a contractor. "Marilyn, we'd like you to play assistant concertmaster for *Madame Butterfly*."

"I'd love to, Bob." I was thrilled at this opportunity to perform Puccini's masterpiece again. However, remembering engagements I had taken too soon, I felt the need to caution him.

"Bob, I'm operating on half steam. It's a little difficult to play just now." I did not elaborate. I was still reticent to describe my life to an acquaintance, a colleague.

"Whatever you say, Marilyn. Your standards are high. I'm sure you'll be fine."

Since I had performed the concertmaster solos in the past, I thought the piece would come back to me. Nevertheless, the rehearsal and performance was difficult. I felt detached from myself, as if someone else were playing. The stress of my double life on dialysis had taken away my sense of normalcy. I was relieved to reach the end of the performance and realized I could not function in this state. I must have presented a face of competence because my colleagues complimented me. I felt like an impostor, barely hanging on. After this experience, I resigned myself to low-pressure performances such as weddings and parties.

We started to test for the transplant. An abdominal sonogram revealed that my internal organs were in place and functioning properly. As a preparation for acceptance of my father's kidney I was given his blood in three transfusions to insure that antibodies would not be formed against it. The preliminary transfusions were a new procedure that decreased the risk of rejection. During one dialysis, I took cyclosporine to test my reaction to the drug. Immediately my blood pressure rose and I broke out in a rash. From this reaction, it was obvious that my body required prednisone along with cyclosporine.

During the years after kidney failure, when lupus was in remission, I had been free of prednisone. This was a happy event. A side effect of kidney failure, at least for me, was this wonderful cessation of lupus. I felt that my spiritual preparation had paved the way for this, but it was also possible that catastrophic kidney failure was the last kick in the butt this disease dealt before it finished with me.

In reply to my frantic questions about the prednisone I would have to take after the transplant, the doctors explained that eventually a dosage of only ten milligrams a day would be required. This amount replaced what adrenal glands normally produce. I had wrestled with cortisone for twenty-one years. After the transplant, I would be required to take it every day for the rest of my life. Though this mandate tempted me to reconsider the transplant, I was discovering that life would require compromises and the weighing of options.

Since the only alternative, dialysis, was not an option, I accepted these conditions. Other drugs included immuran (another immunosuppressant like prednisone which I had used to treat lupus flares in the past), the moderate blood pressure reducing drugs clonidine and procardia XL, and cyclosporine to prevent rejection of the foreign organ.

I was horrified at the prospect of imbibing this cornucopia of pharmaceuticals. My cheeks would fill out. My stomach would become round and my legs spindly. I would lose the look that I thought of as me. I worried that the familiar feeling that accompanied prednisone would be difficult to live with, though I was comforted at the low dosage of ten milligrams. The prednisone, along with immuran and my spiritual work, would probably keep lupus away forever. I consoled myself with this. Though the cost of these drugs was prohibitive, fortunately, our musician's union drug plan saved us.

October 30, 1990, the date we had chosen for the transplant, drew near. I began cyclosporine and prednisone therapy and continued my inner preparation toward the success of the operation. Wimberly had kept her sister's kidney for ten years. She had struggled with early dialysis methods for years before she received her kidney. Wimberly and her sister Susan's tissue match had been like twins. As my mentor, she advised me to focus on positive results regardless of the statistical probabilities.

One night, while sorting through information to effect my final decision, I called her. I was still holding out for a natural solution. I might be taking a fatal chance, but it seemed necessary to make this final effort.

"You know, Marilyn, I was also seeking cures just before my transplant. I continued to believe the natural method might be my salvation rather than opting for drug dependence the rest of my life."

"What did you do?"

"I found this clinic in Arizona and made an appointment to see the director. He was uninterested in my condition. He seemed egotistical and almost rude. I decided that I would not trust this person with my life. I left immediately and went home to prepare for the transplant. I've never regretted it."

I was stunned. What a coincidence! My father had offered to sponsor a trip to an Arizona healing center, at the same clinic I was considering! That settled it. No questions remained. I would not risk death in the hands of a charlatan again. Wimberly had done my research for me. I could not believe my good luck. Now I could proceed with a clear conscience.

My doctors informed me that the success of the operation relied on the ability of my body to accept a foreign organ as its own. This is not an assured process. My chances for success were dependent on several factors—tissue matches and my state of health. Focusing on the positive outcome of my transplant was like walking a mental tightrope. I refused to allow statistics of organ rejection to cloud my thinking. The pervasive fear in the transplant community was that the dreaded numbers of high creatinine clearance indicated that the new kidney was failing. It was terrifying to think that my lifeline, my new kidney, could give up, and I would be back on dialysis. When thoughts of this possibility intruded, I focused all my mental energy to disallow this panic and walk the straight and narrow path of faith.

Many feel they are living in the real world only when they know all the facts. Statistics are certainly important, but there is little emphasis on how a recipient uses the information. Can a patient obsess over the outcome to the eventual failure of the procedure? Absolutely. I have seen it happen. I have watched several lose their new kidneys as they anxiously awaited each day's test results, unaware that the surfeit of facts they were processing clouded their ability to concentrate on a right outcome. The mind will direct the body successfully if given a chance, but it must be guided to correct results. I decided that my happy result hinged on unswerving faith.

The week before the surgery I played flute and violin duets with Sheryl Henze. It seemed that someone else was drawing the bow across the strings and I was watching from somewhere among the rafters. The Sunday before my operation I played concertmaster for a small group at a church on the East Side. I felt like a fraud in this position of authority. Afterwards my friend Marya invited me to her loft in Soho. We took the subway downtown and decided to shop at a friend's clothing store. I was excited at the prospect of doing something fun, but I was so weak that I could barely walk a block. Sinking into a parish bench near the front door, I watched Marya try on clothes. At her five-story walkup loft, somehow, I found the strength to negotiate the stairs. Breathing heavily, I flopped on their Indian bedspread while they read the Sunday Times. We shared a relaxed afternoon in their sunlit, plant-filled loft as Marya and Ron allowed me to rest before I summoned the strength to go home. Though my friends were kind to me, their frame of reference was different from my own. Again I felt the familiar gap stretch between myself and my healthy friends.

Diana Smith-Barker was another friend who did not shrink from the gritty details of my illness. Her husband had died of cancer at the age of 33. Tom's tragic death had given her a familiarity with the health-care system. Diana was a devout Quaker. The Christian ideal of compassionate caring was not just a theory to her. Her friendship was invaluable to me.

The night before my operation the nurses warned me that I might not come out of surgery alive. I signed my surgery agreement recognizing the risks involved. During moments of weakness I was terrified that the procedure might fail, yet I was full of expectation for the new life that awaited me. I was also concerned for Dad. He was over seventy. If complications arose, I did not want to be responsible for my father's death.

While I was dialyzed in M-2 for (hopefully) the last time, Diana read from the Book of Psalms. She played her violin. We sang hymns. Her love gave me the strength to face what was to come. The dialysis nurses shared our joy, delighted to hear a free concert that lightened their somber chores. I could feel their support. I finished my dialysis without a tuna sandwich this night. I did not eat before the surgery. Exhausted but excited, I waited for the catheter to be removed, then for the nurse's thumb pressure to stop the bleeding. Through it all, Diana sat quietly by my side. I rested in her love and the certainty that the Father was giving His love to me. I shall never forget the sweet anticipation of that night and Diana's kindness, which will remain in my heart forever.

BEGIN

Setting aside the trials
of Yesterday,

Pushing away the fears
for Tomorrow,

I walk the straight and
narrow path
of Today.

Not easy,
yet the simplest
of all things.
Strive without strife,
Love without self,
Be without fear;
Ever being retaught.
When all that is required
is to
Begin.

—Marilyn Gibson

XX.

The Transplant

My father entered the New York Hospital the day before the surgery. He went to the seventh floor while I went to the kidney transplant wing near M-2. It was a cheerful place, filled with hope for a new life. Here in one of the finest transplant units in the world, medical miracles happened every day. Though I knew the success probability was good for living related donors, doubts still assailed me. I tried not to entertain them and concentrated instead on the straight and narrow path of successful outcomes.

My roommate Julie and I gazed curiously at each other from our beds. Julie had been on CAPD for several years. Her family was a close-knit Italian clan, each of whom had volunteered a kidney. She chose her little sister's.

"So, how did you feel about CAPD?" I asked curiously.

"It was easy. I work as a sports writer. Near my office, there is a room where I can change my bags. The people there are great. My family is supportive, too. I live at home, you see."

I listened to her, nodding. Her description of CAPD made it seem simple, though I knew it was not. She was swarthy, with brown eyes and short brown hair. Her countenance was calm, while I could not stop feeling agitated. She spoke quietly, almost in a monotone. I wondered if she was capable of anxiety. She must have devised some secret method of dealing with this, I thought. Possibly, she had been on dialysis so long that she had become immune to medical procedures. When she mentioned her low blood pressure, I thought that this must be her secret, with a twinge of envy. High blood pressure had plagued me since kidney failure.

My sleep the night before the operation was sporadic, but this was normal in a hospital. Besides, our room was adjacent to the nurse's station, where something was always going on. Finally, the big day dawned. Slightly before six, after donning a clean gown and a hair net, I was transferred to a stretcher. I was wheeled through the corridors to an elevator that transported me up to the surgical ward. The nurses and doctors wore a strange shade of aquamarine used for 'scrub' attire. The ward was gleaming and bustling with energy. Just outside the operating room, I noted a sign-up list for a stress-reduction group. Here real lives were at stake. It was not like the embarrassment of playing a wrong note in Carnegie Hall, though that could be stressful, too.

I was surprised at how small the operating room seemed, but I barely had time to register my reaction to my surroundings. With dispatch, I was transferred onto the cold operating table. Immediately the anesthesiologists connected three lines from an artery in my neck to their machine.

"This won't be enough," a bespectacled face peered at me upside down. "How about the right arm?"

"Her shunt is there."

"Oh. Let's try her ankle." They started another IV in my ankle. I felt like a pincushion, but soon I would not even notice.

The anesthesiologist bustled into the room. "Are you comfortable?" he asked.

"Sort of," an uneasy laugh escaped.

"Okay, then. Count back from 100."

I got to 97 and I was out. I did not see the surgeon at all.

Meanwhile, in an adjacent operating room, Darracott Vaughn, my father's surgeon, had already begun. After the anesthesia took effect, a foot-long incision was made across Dad's back and his right kidney was removed. It was carried to my operating room, where an incision had been made just over my right ovary. I was later told that I would still be able to wear a bikini after the surgery. Many believe that the kidneys are removed in a transplant operation, a procedure that is unnecessary and terribly painful. After the operation, I would have three kidneys and my father would have one.

Afterwards I awakened in the Recovery Room feeling like a gutted animal. At the fringes of my awareness, I heard a small child crying. The incision, kept together by copper staples, was my only thought. An intravenous morphine drip made the pain tolerable. I felt chilly and began to shake. A nurse hovered around me, covering me with heated blankets that she replaced frequently. I was flattered by the attention, realizing that she was tending solely to me.

After a four-hour stay in the recovery room, I returned to the kidney ward, where I barely survived the next twenty-four hours. My first recollection was a shifting black-and-white geometric image. I was watching a kaleidoscopic M. C. Escher print inside my head. I had never experienced this sensation before, even on pulse therapy. Soon I began to receive unfamiliar psychic messages. I was assimilating a new organ and its DNA codes as well as spiritual aspects connected to my new kidney.

I recalled a film in which a transplanted murderer's hand became an instrument for murder in the new body. Though this scenario is implausible, I can attest that some transference does take place. My father joked that I inherited his "good old Republican kidney". Though my politics had not changed, I did feel a new surge of energy and optimism. This was due in part to new iron in my blood, but it was also my father's approach to life. His kidney had transferred a new sanguinity to me. This wonderful enthusiasm would soon become an integral part of my new life.

Learning how to breathe again was not easy after my lungs had been shut down for hours. Every hour on the hour I was required to turn over and cough. After each tiny cough a small gauge, as those used to assess the air in tires, estimated my breathing capacity. My coughs sounded like burps. The staples over the incision did not help either. In addition, I had become seriously anemic. I would require three blood transfusions before the night was over.

A resident decided to inject potassium into my bloodstream. My body became a white-hot flame. I thought I would die immediately, but I clenched my fists and prayed the agony would pass. Around three a.m. the nurses decided I should sit up in bed. I sat up and spewed the bouillon I had forced down earlier. The scene was right out of *The Exorcist*. In spite of their urging, I never made it out of the bed into a chair that night.

Though originally scheduled first, Julie got Dr. Steubenbord's second transplant slot. She seemed to experience none of the complications that I had and slept placidly through this hellish night. I again marveled at her equanimity. Finally, the first light of dawn sifted through my window, In this new day I gained more optimism than I had possessed in years.

It was Halloween. This is truly the first day of the rest of my life, I thought, as electric energy surged through me. I felt as if I had awakened from a long, deep sleep. Julie and I smiled conspiratorially. We were one of medicine's greatest triumphs. When Tim arrived for his daily visit, the atmosphere on the ward was festive. I joined in, sitting up in my bed and taking calls from friends and relatives.

My new kidney was jump-started with intravenous glucose. After my IV was disconnected, I was instructed to drink as much water as I could hold—eight glasses every few hours. The two IV's in my neck remained for the first three days, though they pulled the one in my ankle just after the surgery. The volume of my urine output was measured and tested. Reports were good. With the exception of my healthy period of eight-and-a-half-months, I had not had a normal creatinine for almost three years. Now my creatinine hovered around 1.0, a completely normal reading. My blessed new kidney was now excreting toxins that had never been completely cleared with dialysis.

From here on I made astounding progress. I experienced no rejection episodes, unlike many others on the ward. Tim and I were grateful that my mental and physical preparation had paid off. Julie and I were quarantined for the first few days. Flowers were not allowed. Our inhibited immune systems might respond to the microbes lurking inside. At this tender stage, we could not afford an infection. The flowers that did arrive were transferred to the nurses' station, which must have been a fragrant area indeed.

The nurses at New York Hospital's kidney ward were exceptional. Especially the head nurse, a tiny blonde with long beautiful hair. Surprisingly efficient and tough, she reminded me of my cousin Teresa.

The atmosphere on the ward was friendly and optimistic. Only a few years ago we would have been dead. In the early years of dialysis, hemodialysis required eight hours instead of four. Shunts were less reliable and were shifted from place to place, creating patchwork arms. Access to the machines was limited. Medical workers found themselves in the impossible position of choosing who would dialyze and who would die. We were the lucky ones, benefiting from the accomplishments and sacrifices of those who came before. Having been given this precious gift of hope, I vowed that my life would never be wasted. I would be thankful for every minute on earth with health and vitality.

I began to take the immunosuppressant drugs that I would need for the rest of my life. I took cyclosporine, prednisone and immuran for suppression of my immune system, so that my body would not reject the foreign kidney. I took clonidine and procardia XL for blood pressure, though in a much smaller dosage than I had been required to take while on dialysis. The new kidney kept my blood pressure closer to normal. At first, I retained my 'skinny face'. I had not taken prednisone for three years; I had not needed it on dialysis. My restricted, unappetizing diet had resulted in a thin figure. I got a pixie haircut before the operation, short in front and long in back. I was pleased with my appearance although I was yellow from the beginnings of long-term dialysis coloration.

However, it was only a matter of time before the moon-face would manifest itself. My yellow caste would soon disappear and rosy cortisone-cheeks would replace it. On the day of the surgery, I was given 100 milligrams, but it was quickly tapered down. A prolonged period of at least two weeks was required to create the moon-face. It probably would not appear until I left the hospital.

Two friends came to visit. One was Stanley Bednar, the head of the string department at my alumnus, the Manhattan School of Music. As he walked into my room I was flooded with memories of that day, almost twenty years ago, when I played the Dvorak concerto for the jury he chaired. Stanley was probably instrumental in getting approval for my full scholarship. I was amazed to see him, and even more stunned to learn that his brother had received a kidney transplant. After the operation, his brother had traveled the world. During the dark days from which I had barely emerged, it was impossible to travel without prohibitive obstacles. I was thrilled to hear of such freedom.

Wimberly accompanied him. She looked fantastic. Tall and dark, she wore a conservative maroon cardigan and plaid skirt. "You're so slim," she said, holding my hand.

"Not for long," I laughed. "As you know, the prednisone affects my appetite. Food tastes delicious! I can finally eat what I want! I must try all the foods I've been denied for so long."

"I can understand that," she agreed. "As soon as I returned from the hospital I hit every pastrami deli I could find. Things got out of hand and I put on some weight, so I took it off through Weight Watchers. Even now, the weight goes on my stomach first. It is a constant struggle."

I nodded, happy that these two special people had come to lend their support. After they left, my spirits continued to soar. After visiting hours, when Tim had gone home, Julie and I shared more information about our lives. She was unfamiliar with classical music so I played her some Berlioz on my CD player and she was surprised to discover that she really liked it. I continued to marvel at her even nature when we played cards to pass the time. One day while we were playing gin rummy she slipped and fell from her chair. Several alarmed nurses rushed to her aid. Soon afterward, she experienced a rejection episode.

On the third day after the transplant, I enjoyed a normal diet! For breakfast, I ordered eggs, sausage, bagel, pancakes, and cream cheese. There was no salt restriction for the first time in three years. The blood pressure problem equalized as the new kidney took over. It was easy for me to overindulge. This was my first hospital stay with cause for celebration. I thought this must be what having a baby would be like—looking forward to leaving the hospital with something beautiful instead of departing decimated and dazed.

Though I was anxious about the results of my creatinine tests like everyone else, I kept my emotions in check. The doctors were thrilled with the successful results. A third patient moved into the room next to the nurses' station to join Julie and me. Her husband had donated his kidney. He was a laborer, tall and muscular. He admired my father, whom he had met on the donor's ward upstairs. "That man is a bull!" he exclaimed. "Looks like he isn't a day over fifty!"

I was doing well, but Julie was still having complications. She remained in our intensive care room next to the nurses' station while I moved across the hall to a four-bed room. Fortunately, I got a windowed cubicle. The patient in the bed across from mine had been in a coma for a month. Miraculously, she had regained consciousness. I was impressed with her indomitable spirit. While in a coma, she had had a colostomy. Now she was too weak to walk but was gaining strength. She was around fifty and her Japanese husband must have been at least twenty years younger. On a few occasions, he brought sushi as a special treat. I loved sushi. It was my favorite food. Yet, when he offered me some, I refused. At this stage of my recovery, I did not want to take a chance on microbes in the raw fish.

The doctors seemed to respect the success of my transplant coupled with my feisty, hands-on attitude about my care. One day, deciding I felt much better, I donned a beautiful nightgown and robe that had been a present from Doris, my father's fiancée. Richly embellished in shades of purple, ruby and emerald, my attire seemed to inspire new respect from the staff. I was puzzled. Maybe the opulent colors affected them—or possibly, it was my emerging sense of power. I did feel transformed, and the tangible difference in the treatment I received seemed to reinforce this metamorphosis.

Exercise was encouraged, so I trekked up and down the hall as far as the dialysis unit. At the end of the hall was the M-2 pavilion. After each lap of my walk I arrived at the dialysis unit and peeked in at the poor wretches who were hooked up to machines. A part of me was still terrified that I would rejoin them. However, I would not allow that fear to take hold. Instead I focused on my new health and worked even harder to build my stamina, starting with thirty laps, then forty, then up to a hundred times a day. Though the incision was painful, it was a joy to walk with gusto. I delighted in the energy that surged through me like a mighty river. Julie chose not to exercise. I felt this was sacrificing her recovery. Her complacency now appeared to be a lack of the will to live.

My father had come through admirably, though he had picked up a staph infection at the hospital. Not yet well enough to travel to Virginia, he was released after a few days. He returned to my apartment although he came to visit several times.

The male transplant nurses often showed movies in the evenings. We gathered in our robes in the spacious, peach-colored lounge adjacent to M-2 when the ward was quiet. A handsome cabinet that housed a huge television and VCR was wheeled out. Our raw emotions meshed well with the bittersweet love story *Always* starring Richard Dreyfuss and

Holly Hunter. A beautiful friendship had developed between us. We were given the gift of life after so much suffering.

One of my new friends was a schoolteacher whose husband had donated his kidney. They had a young son. Her creatinine hovered around two, which was a little high. Each day we waited anxiously as the creatinine results came in. I felt sorry that she was experiencing complications and could not go home.

Another woman was a journalist. She had been in the ward for a month and was not recovering as expected. Dr. Steubenbord came to see her every day. I sensed his concern. He did not want to give up hope, but the cadaver kidney was not working. Finally, he gave the dreaded order of dialysis. Before her transplant, she had been on dialysis for nine years. I wondered if this length of time had decreased her chances for success. Everyone on the ward was hoping for the transplant to work. Her boyfriend visited infrequently. More often, her mother came. Occasionally my walks to M-2 would correspond with her dialysis time, and I often overheard them fighting. The uncertainty must have been dreadful. It was sad that her boyfriend was not more reliable. I was grateful that Tim had taken responsibility for me. During dire circumstances, a matrimonial bond can provide the extra glue a couple needs to survive.

Another man down the hall had diabetes and was hovering around rejection after receiving a cadaver kidney. His anxiety kept him in a state of agitation. One night he bothered the nurses at the station next to my room every few minutes with a different request or question. I wanted to say, "Relax. It will increase your chances of success." The next day a walk-man was stolen from his room and he became even more agitated. I feared he might worry himself out of his transplant. I felt fortunate to have averted this self-destructive path. I could not imagine going through this deeply traumatic procedure again. Many dialysis patients had rejected two or three transplants. I marveled at these veterans who steeled themselves repeatedly for the painful surgery in hopes for a new life.

One evening almost at midnight my favorite dialysis nurse stopped by my room after her shift.

"You look wonderful!" she exclaimed as she grasped my hand. "How do you feel?"

"Better than I have for a long time."

"It is a miracle," she smiled. "Best of luck to you."

After she left, I marveled at the happiness I felt. I was so grateful to this woman. She had helped me to survive and savor this moment. Yes, she was right. It was a miracle, and she was one of my angels. M-2 was only down the hall, yet it seemed light years away.

XXI.

Home

On November 10, 1990, eleven days after the transplant, I left the New York Hospital. It was a comforting womb, but the time had come to emerge into my new life. Sadly, I bade farewell to the other hopefuls on the ward. We had shared so much. Our transplant fraternity was an unbroken line stretching across the world. I was filled with love for my new brothers and sisters, each of whom understood what it was like to face death and return to vitality.

Visits to Rogosin, where my creatinine was closely monitored, were frequent. I was not to work for three months and forbidden to lift heavy objects. November passed quickly. My prednisone was tapered and by December, I was down to 25 milligrams a day.

Tim was hired to play bamboo flute in the in the orchestra for the Broadway show *Shogun*. After that time, he joined the orchestra of *Miss Saigon*. Our financial picture was looking up. On December 10, just after my arrival home, we shared in the birth of four kittens. Our white angora, Bunny was the mother. Three were born at first, and then a fourth was born three hours later. Their eyes were closed and their ears pasted to their heads. They swayed back and forth like drunken sailors in their first awkward steps around the birthing box. Their paws had miniature pink pads with little extended claws. Each morning I carefully lifted them out of their box and played with them. Their father

Bubby (a black shorthair) surprised us by jumping in their box and grooming them as Bunny did. At first, I feared that they could be harmed, but they bonded to him. This joyful event made my recuperation time go a lot faster.

My father and Doris stayed in the bedroom of our one-bedroom apartment while we slept on the hide-a-bed in the living room. Doris was a nervous person. Though she tried to be helpful, New York City eluded her. She was lost easily and found traffic intimidating. Each time she left the apartment I worried about her. Tim, working on the flute parts for *Miss Saigon,* needed time to practice alone. Doris was usually in the bedroom of our one-bedroom apartment with Dad. Each time Tim started to practice, she would emerge into the living room.

"Tim, could you play a little number for me? I love the flute—always have." She sat on the couch and waited to be entertained.

"Doris, I'd love to, but I have work to do."

"Well, all right, then. I know when I'm not wanted," she said, storming into the bedroom. The tension in the apartment seemed to affect Dad's healing time. His staph infection refused to improve and I was afraid I might pick it up. The immumosuppressant drugs made me vulnerable. Quarters were cramped, but I was determined not to let the situation upset me. I had come too far to sacrifice the success of my operation to stress at home.

Most of the time I also stayed in the apartment. I ventured out only to Riverside Park. My father and I took long walks. We discussed the nature of things and speculated on the world situation, just as we had since I was a child. We had always shared a special relationship, but this sacrifice strengthened our bond. I would always be in his debt for the gift of love he had given me. I was determined that the rest of my life would count. Not only would I savor the privilege of a healthy life, but also I would use my new vitality to create joy for those around me.

My focus had changed. Today, and every day for the rest of my life, I would concentrate on gratitude for my blessings. I had arisen from the dead. If that wasn't cause for celebration, what was?

On December 17, I went back to work playing the violin. Tim drove me to the rehearsal, held in the basement of the Turtle Bay Music School. Our small orchestra accompanied the Beethoven First Piano Concerto. I felt fragile and new in reentering this world. Many of my colleagues did not know I had a transplant, and I kept it a secret from all except those who inquired.

On a Christmas Eve midnight service at the Madison Avenue Presbyterian Church, I performed first violin in a string quartet. In this solo context, it was difficult to conceal my fragility. I was so nervous that my bow arm shook as I drew it across the string. I was certain that the audience could hear, but I found that it had not been obvious to anyone but me. In spite of my nervousness, playing beautiful music again was a sweet reward.

I substituted for one of the violinists at *Shogun*. It was a dream come true. I had always wanted to work on Broadway. Though the moon-face had appeared, I did not mind. I would have to live with it for the rest of my life anyway. The tradeoff was healthy vitality with energy to do my work. No more anemia. No more starvation. I was a little more susceptible to infections and bruised easily, but this was a small price to pay compared to dialysis. Those who forget their lessons are doomed to repeat them, I often reminded myself.

I did not need lupus in my life any more. I reasoned that after the disease had socked me with kidney failure, it was finished with me. Moreover, immuran and prednisone were probably prophylactic. In addition to these obvious reasons, my new kidney provided a tide of energy. Through right use of will, I was able to direct my life force correctly. Energy was no longer a finite quantity to be conserved through rest. I now seemed to have unlimited resources. Releasing the old mental habits of negativity was also helpful. As I returned to my profession, I reminded myself not to succumb to fear. Fears of success or failure were components of stress. It would not be realistic to say that these emotions dropped away in important performance situations. I merely put them in perspective of life and death. Failure could not compare to any of the life-threatening situations I had survived, and certainly it was trivial compared to dialysis.

Unfortunately, *Shogun* was short-lived, but soon after it closed, Tim began rehearsals for Miss *Saigon*, which was a big hit. During that period, Tim often spoke of LouAnn, the show's concertmaster. He respected her professionalism and musicianship. When he had performed at *Phantom of the Opera* as a sub, she had been impressed with his beautiful sound and had recommended him for *Saigon*. We owed her a tremendous debt. One night I came to pick up Tim outside the Broadway stage door. When she emerged in a red scarf that set off her beautiful blonde hair, I sensed a woman of great strength.

"Marilyn, this is Lou Ann," Tim said.

"I've heard so much about you," she said warmly. "It is a pleasure to meet you at last."

Her graceful dignity impressed me. A few days later she called me to substitute for her at a *Miss Saigon* rehearsal. I could not believe my good fortune. During a break in the rehearsal, I tripped on a step. Quickly regaining my balance, I caught my breath. I could have lost my transplant just as I was getting started again! I vowed to be more careful. Soon afterwards I again played *Miss Saigon* and soon became a regular sub. LouAnn, a wonderful artist and person, made this opportunity for success possible.

The self-knowledge gained from my spiritual search now enabled me to place myself in work situations that were not injurious to my sense of self-esteem. My tendency in the past had been to discount my abilities, believing deep in my heart that I was unworthy of success. Clearing this illusion allowed me to work toward achieving my life's goals. I now had new stamina and optimism and vowed to prove myself worthy of the great gift I had been given.

XXII.

Modern Medical Science and Healing

I am living a normal life today because of the valiant efforts of dedicated and intelligent medical professionals. However, I also suspect that lupus itself may be in significant degree **caused** by modern medical science. I believe that lupus is a disease of the twentieth century. Though the disease was not well-known in 1959 when my mother was diagnosed, after lupus and other chronic diseases have been documented for several decades, the promised cure has not materialized. Why is this? I believe it is because we are entering a new era in the understanding of disease in which we will master the mind-body connection. This is the next step in our evolution. That is why the 'magic bullet' will never be found for chronic diseases. It exists within us.

In our new Millennium, many of our concepts are changing. Established systems are breaking down as they fail to supply our needs. The direction of this change mandates that we acknowledge the role of spirit in healing. Even the most conservative medical establishments are now recommending preventive healing through gentler herb therapy, meditation for reduction of stress, and intelligent diet and exercise choices. Also, when exorbitant medical bills and horrifying side effects drive people away from ineffectual and sometimes even toxic treatment, they become motivated to seek preventive methods which will keep them out of the doctor's office.

Today researchers are endeavoring to find a 'magic bullet' which will cure lupus. However, with chronic diseases, the parameters are more unpredictable. Infectious diseases are simpler. The virus or bacteria is located and eliminated. Lupus, the great pretender, is a more sophisticated adversary. When lupus sets the body against itself, antibodies are made as if a foreign bacteria or virus is invading it. The body may be misinterpreting signals brought on by a number of causes: toxic overexposure to prescription drugs, stimulation of the adrenal glands through fear and guilt emotions, or other imbalances. Genetic factors may provide a weakness for the disease that manifests itself when stressors weaken the organism.

I believe that thought patterns held in opposition to the flow of life causes disease. Physical symptoms are usually the last result. Lupus symptoms slowed me down during the summer session, just as I was preparing to get ahead of the competition by attending summer school. It is possible that my rush for competitive victory caused severe guilt reactions. Swelling in my feet and fingers slowed my quest for violin mastery. This gave me a convenient excuse not to practice. I was impatient, not willing to let the growth process proceed naturally. There was so much to accomplish. The fear of failure was a pervasive motivation for me at that time. A healthy fear can spur one to achieve a glorious performance, but I had not learned how to use this fear constructively. The initial flare of lupus may have been initiated by sulfa drug therapy, but it was formed over time through fear and guilt reactions held as continual thought patterns.

Before the manifestation of hemolytic anemia there were months of strain caused by a dysfunctional marriage. This was very painful. Again, I internalized my unhappiness. After a recovery period during which I became more familiar with myself and past dependency patterns, I met and married Tim. Yet, even as I thought I had made progress toward self-sufficiency, I allowed myself to loosen a control that had served me well while living alone. This is a typical condition for women today, but was even more common in past generations. The example of my mother was one I subconsciously repeated. She pursued music, her greatest love, only as an avocation and performed secretarial work to support the family. I believe my mother suffered for her decisions. Though she would never have admitted it, I could see that she internalized this suffering. I believe it manifested physically as lupus. I encouraged my mother to exercise, but she resisted. As her energy was diverted through health crises, she missed opportunities for her full realization. When the slow downward spiral of her disease began, this avenue of expression left her in painful increments. She longed to enjoy the full realization of her talents, but in the end, her disease was the victor.

Although I had searched myself with brutal honesty, lying bare a lifetime of physical and emotional habits that may have caused 'my' disease, the doctors at each hospital admission asked the same questions. Their questions took into consideration none of these elements. I cooperated, realizing that gathering information was a necessity if they were to cure me of the disorders I had created. It is true that the causes above are not quantifiable. If scientists were to accept my premises, they would find themselves attempting to define parameters for which they would have no frame of reference. However, the source of my frustration with them was that these causative elements were completely unacknowledged.

Thus I maintained my separate life of discovery, never daring to cross the invisible line which separates the unseen and thus unquantifiable from the accepted modes of treatment. During my hospital stays, I accepted the regime that measured the extent to which my body had strayed from normal health. In crises, these causative factors seemed irrelevant, but I believe they were not in my case. It seemed apparent to me that the inner causes were as important in formulating a cure as they were in forming the disease. Because of this belief, I struggled to maintain my spiritual focus as an aid to healing.

If we possessed the full awareness to which we are evolving, perhaps the mind could heal without drugs. However, this skill will only be developed through an intimate knowledge of our connection to the vast power of which we are merely fragments. Unfortunately, the omnipresent medicalization of healing impedes us by viewing disease as an entity detached from its cause, and a great chance for understanding is lost. Treatment should entail the caregiver working in collaboration with life's greater source rather than ignoring its existence.

Some would say that physical reality is the only reliable means of understanding the world around us. However, I believe that in the healing of lupus and other chronic diseases we need a combination of these methods. The patient's personal history must include a detailed psychological assessment of all factors leading to the manifestation of symptoms. Crises should be avoided *before they occur* and to rid oneself of toxic accumulations both physical and mental.

Although mastery of emotions will be our next step in healing, the most powerful healing force is Love. When life has gone awry through distressing illness, the sufferer must begin a painfully honest assessment of her/himself. In the future, I believe we will develop talented healing professionals who will see into the heart of the sufferer, who will aid the patient's healing through Love. However, each individual must take responsibility for his healing. Self-hate, fear and guilt must be released. This is a long process, but ultimately very rewarding. By clearing away the many grudges that have lodged like barnacles in the patient's body and soul, these methods can banish most stress-related diseases.

Concepts of a limited good health, which is dependent upon the medical establishment for cures, and other limiting beliefs are foisted upon us constantly through the media, which reinforces negative emotions of anger, hate and fear and their painful results. Because of their powerful influence, negative messages in the nightly news and newspapers must be avoided during the time of healing. The patient must develop concentration and the ability to divorce her/himself from manipulation, at least during the time of spiritual regeneration. This will make the healing process easier.

If a doctor's care is required because a crisis exists or is forming, drugs such as prednisone arrest symptoms beautifully, and antibiotics save lives. We are indeed lucky to have such powerful tools. After the symptoms are arrested, however, the victim must remain vigilant and refer to his honest assessment of their emotional and spiritual causes, or they will manifest again.

Our life-force energy must be expressed. If it is not used creatively it will be turned outward through violence or inward through disease, which is violence to ourselves. If we nurture our beings with loving kindness, we are empowered to create a glorious world where we interact with one another and learn. As we grow in knowledge, the fear of connection to the vast force that sustains us will drop away. Instead, we will embrace this beautiful energy as we learn to channel it.

The Law of Life is Love. We were created in Love and were born to express Love. Our work is Love made manifest. We must find work that allows the life force to flow outward unimpeded. The healer Jesus Christ magnified the force of Love, channeling the vast creative force of the Universe so that His supplicants were healed instantly. As astounding as were His miraculous deeds, He promised, "The works that I do, ye shall do also, and greater." What an exciting idea! Have we pondered these words? Do we really recognize their significance?

We are each endowed with limitless power. The blinding light from which we came is waiting to be expressed in each one of us. We have allowed the light to be veiled through delusion and ignorance. We are finding our way back. It is our destiny to heal ourselves. The most powerful drug can heal only if the patient allows it. Health is our normal state, intended for us to enjoy. If we place full faith in our healing it will manifest to some degree, and we will experience the joy of spiritual cleansing in the process.

XXIII.

An End to Suffering

Created in God's image, we have dominion over the creatures of the earth. However, we have misused our power with horrible consequences. We have exploited or eliminated too many of the species with which we share our planet. Through our uncontrolled propagation, we are destroying the very air we breathe and water we drink. If we were truly evolved, we would not kill our own and every other species irresponsibly. Nor would we feel envy, greed, guilt, anger or fear—so often the emotions of separation. There would be no disease, which is the malfunctioning of the organism. We could decree the transfer of our eternal souls to the next dimension. We could create new life forms by willing them into manifestation. We could float freely between dimensions and change our own forms. We would function in complete harmony with others, relating to them through joy and love. Our scope of awareness would expand to include mind groups through which we share common commitment and ideals. The family would be redefined to include larger sections of humanity.

Masters past and present actually possess these powers. Many who have passed on have opted to return as an act of sacrifice. Though they are capable of dwelling in the heaven-like environments they have earned, they often return to help humanity to its next stage of evolution. During my vision near death, a loving master guided me. I was evaluated compassionately by an ascended being who had much greater knowledge than I could comprehend. Although I had created a powerful hell on earth through my disease experiences, my near-death experience was a blissful heaven.

In my near-death experience, it was indicated that the psychic environment I inhabited on earth would be similar to my destination after leaving this body. The loving master who beckoned at the end of the Golden Tunnel urged me to leave this world, but it was a gentle call. The information necessary to choose my actions was presented as a choice for my Divine Soul.

The great religions of Judaism, Hinduism, Christianity, Buddhism and Islam give us rules which lead us to the end of suffering; we are directed to maintain our physical, mental and spiritual bodies. I believe it is essential that we direct a portion of our considerable energies to understanding these concepts and working to attain spiritual advancement. By gaining control over our spiritual selves, we will begin to develop powers like those of the Masters. We will find that the world we inhabit is full of joy, even on the physical plane. If, however, we choose to ignore the universal laws we must face the consequences through suffering.

Our selfish or ignorant behavior can create untold misery. I experienced an apparition from the dark side the night my kidneys failed. I envisioned the inhabitant of my own hell in his dynamic refusal to acknowledge a higher force. He avoided the light that draws one's soul away from the earth dimension at the time of death. The fear of death in our culture stems from this lack of continuity. We have yet to accept the reincarnation theory as they do in the East. In denying it, we cut ourselves off from a comforting premise. If this life is the only existence, it may spur us to accomplish great things; or it may encourage us to take no responsibility for future generations. How much more comforting is it to believe that we travel to a beautiful world of spirit at the time of death. Then, with the knowledge of this most recent life tucked away, we rest for awhile before we re-form into a new soul. Then, if necessary, armed with new understanding, we plunge back into this school of earth for an entirely new experience.

Metaphysicians call our physical body a vehicle. They believe that our Higher Self, or Divine Soul, remains the same but creates and sheds new bodies as we evolve. I have seen images of myself in past lives as both a man and a woman. I have seen my cat Bunny as a lion in a past life. These visions have convinced me that we are indeed evolving through each life. Our animals are evolving, too. When I despair that magnificent animal species are dying, I recall my vision and am comforted that the soul of a big cat is now dwelling in Bunny.

The spiritual masters and saints who have attained control of the physical function on higher levels, or vibrations, and influence other beings there. Returning to those on earth through dreams or visions, they bring messages of hope and inspiration and assist in healings and spiritual growth. Dwelling in the frequency of Love, they bestow their blessings to all that ask. For those of us on a spiritual path, this is a goal of our present development.

Every human on earth feels the need to return to the oneness from which she came. Though this happens naturally at death, we often feel a lack stemming from our feelings of separation. Enlightened masters, saints and angels feel compassion for suffering beings, but they know that all must travel the route to self-knowledge, as they did. All must find their Middle Way.

This is our task. It begins with an honest acceptance of our personal level of evolvement. No one jumps levels to mastery. We each possess a Divine Soul that has all the answers, and we are evolving into greater awareness of that intelligence through learning to control the body and mind.

Nothing is lost. Even in death, we return to the light from which we came and dwell there in full knowledge. A Buddhist concept I have found helpful is to face your karmic debts. That is, if you find yourself in a difficult situation, such as dialysis, embrace it completely in order to move away from it. Accept it as something you have created. Face your fear, the Buddhists say. They warn us that crises must be addressed, if not in this life, then later; so confront them in a dignified way. The more we do this, the sooner we will wipe our karmic slate clean. This will pave the way for entrance into higher mind groups where there is no suffering, only service for the greater good of all.

Many are receiving illness initiations at this time. My experiences have taught me that one's Higher Self could hardly have designed a better method for personal growth. Before I suffered kidney failure, I had begun a zealous spiritual quest. I wanted all the answers at once. Shortly thereafter, enslaved to a machine, I was living through my own personal hell. It was a painful lesson for a willful, independent person to endure. My identity as a violinist was taken away; the physical pleasures of food and water, denied me. I dwelled inside a cage of helpless dependence on that which I loved to hate—the Western materialistic approach.

The view was different there. I had created a profound initiation into the nature of life by setting myself outside of it. With dialysis and the transplant, I gained acceptance of, even gratitude for, those who had graciously saved my life. I learned patience and began to appreciate the miracles I had previously overlooked.

Was it my obstinate refusal to accept a description of symptoms as 'my' disease that brought me to this point? Was it my painful sense of helplessness through each disease crisis? Or my rage at a system which relegated me to the bottom of its hierarchy as a patient? I certainly railed at the ignominious state I had created for myself with each hospitalization, each megadose of prednisone, and each interminable stay in the dialysis chair.

However, I directed this rage into healing energy. With each full recovery, I cooperated with the vast forces regenerating me. The doctors created each miracle with my cooperation. They dissolved insurmountable obstacles and made my recovery possible. I am indebted to them for the gift of life made possible through their dedication and knowledge.

I am continually aware that it is through the largesse of the Creator that I am given time to reside on earth. Each day I ask that I might continue in my quest for a more meaningful life.

I have discovered that the basis of right living is to forge a physical reality from the spiritual. It is not necessary to fight the material approach unless it negates a spiritual source. It is our destiny to create with God because God experiences life through us. We are the tiny sparks which fly from His profound brilliance This is my understanding. If I had not been given lupus erythematosus, I would still be skimming the surface of life, content in my ignorance.

The dialysis phase of my life was a cleansing. While my body was inactive, my mind continually sought the light. I studied metaphysical truths with an unquenchable thirst. When the transplant released me back into vitality, I knew where to direct my new energy. Creativity flowed from me like a mountain stream. Today my transplant is healthy and I have a vibrant, active life. I have discovered that wasteful emotions can be mastered. The sacred gift of life in this dimension is a transcendent opportunity and should never be wasted.

Growth is achieved through many pathways. Mine is only one. We can each make our lives count and make a difference. Just Begin. And continue.

About the Author

Marilyn Gibson plays on Broadway in *Miss Saigon* and *Phantom of the Opera.*

She is the founder and leader of *The Herrick Trio,* which was invited to perform at the *Metropolitan Museum of Art* on their priceless collection of Stradivarius instruments. Ms. Gibson teaches at the premier Suzuki school in the nation, *The School for Strings.* She has written *Soul Songs,* a book of poetry, and *The Light Messengers: Summoning Michael,* a science-fiction novel. She lives in Teaneck, New Jersey with her husband, Tim, two parrots, three finches, a sharpei, a pekingese, and three cats.